Research *and* Development
and the Prospects *for*
International Security

Research *and* Development *and the* Prospects *for* International Security

Frederick Seitz
Rodney W. Nichols

PUBLISHED BY
Crane, Russak &
Company, Inc.
NEW YORK

National Strategy
Information Center, Inc.

Published in the United States by
Crane, Russak & Company, Inc.
347 Madison Avenue
New York, N.Y. 10017

Copyright © 1973 by
National Strategy Information Center, Inc.
130 East 6th Street
New York, N. Y. 10021

Library Edition: ISBN 0-8448-0261-1

Paperbound Edition: ISBN 0-8448-0262-X

LC 73-90816

Strategy Paper No. 22

Printed in the United States of America

Table of Contents

Preface

The US military establishment is currently under sustained attack from several quarters of American opinion. It is variously argued that the armed forces are unnecessarily large for the conduct of policy in a presumed period of international detente, that they are wasteful of scarce human and material resources, and altogether too influential in the formulation of public policy. In this general barrage, expenditures for defense Research and Development are often singled out for special criticism, with the added indictment that overemphasis on defense R&D has seriously damaged and distorted the progress of "peaceful" scientific advance.

The present monograph deals authoritatively with this range of problems in so far as they relate to defense R&D. While accepting the validity of some criticism, the authors argue vigorously against the emasculation of defense R&D in the period ahead, whatever the prospect for real or imagined detente. Their main thesis is that "under the conditions likely to prevail in the future, the pursuit of advanced technology on a selective and imaginative basis affords the United States one of the best guarantees for maintaining international security." Their considered conclusion is that "defense R&D represents a crucial investment toward preserving a margin of safety in deterrence, assuring reliable arms control, and maintaining a credible capability for flexible responses to tactical conflicts that the US cannot ignore."

It would be hard to find two authors more qualified to write on this subject. Dr. Frederick Seitz is President of The Rockefeller University. He began his career as a physicist specializing in the theory of solids and nuclear physics, and had held senior administrative responsibility in many prominent scientific organizations. Dr. Seitz served for many years on the faculty of the University of Illinois, and was President of the National Academy of Sciences for six years before coming to The Rockefeller University in 1968. Rodney W. Nichols, who is a Vice President of the University, began his career as an applied physicist in private industry. During the period 1966-70, he served as Special Assistant for Research and Engineering, Department of Defense. At The Rockefeller University, Mr. Nichols is responsible for planning and development.

Frank R. Barnett, *President*
National Strategy Information Center, Inc.

December 1973

1

Introduction

Presidents Roosevelt, Truman, Eisenhower, Kennedy, and Johnson presided over revolutionary changes in the technologies underlying the foreign and national security policies of the United States. By the end of the 1960s, these policies were under challenge. Scores of new nations had been born in this generation. The international political and economic structure had been transformed by the rise of the Soviet Union to unquestioned superpower status, the emergence of the People's Republic of China, and the recovery and phenomenal economic growth of Japan and West Germany. The once-unrivalled technological leadership of the United States was contested as never before. Under these new conditions, what should be the future relationship between research and development (R&D) and the continuing search for international security?

Technology and technologists are now under attack for many reasons, some valid and some less so. Environmentalists deplore the pollution associated with the industrial applications of modern technology, Humanists fear the dehumanization, the reductionistic mechanization, of work and all other aspects of life. Other critics attack the misuses of technology diverted to "bad" goals. It is argued, for example, that military technology spurs the arms race and drains scarce talent away from urgent civilian tasks.

Some proposals to extend our present technological structure—such as an expansion of the electric power grid—can be analyzed relatively easily and debated on the merits of each case. More novel and imaginative projects are exposed to much broader attack because the potential of advanced systems is less easy to predict. Ironically, this element of unpredictability is one of the reasons why such systems are so interesting to technologists concerned with the beneficial, long-range extension of man's capabilities. The space shuttle, for example, has been heavily criticized because it cannot be demonstrated that this innovation would ultimately be cost-effective —a test that would have ruled out the initial development of the automobile, the airplane, and the electric light. Experience over the past 200 years has shown that several decades of financial support—with farsighted guidance—are usually needed to bring major technological innovations onto the stage in a cost-effective manner. For defense R&D, the assessment of innovations is further complicated by the many uncertainties involved in any projection of political intentions, economic trends, shifting alliances, and the consequences of negotiations.

US defense policies have been dominated for more than a decade by the strategy of nuclear deterrence, which requires the most advanced technology, and by the war in Vietnam, in which the employment of advanced technology was rarely understood, apparently never decisive, and often profoundly questionable. Today, the Soviet Union stands at practical strategic parity with the United States in nuclear arms, and China is rapidly becoming a nuclear power. Strategic deterrence remains essential for our security, while reliable arms control becomes more critical for preserving the narrow margins of stability. In these circumstances, what should be the future role of new strategic technology? And, in light of our withdrawal from Vietnam, and of the Nixon Doctrine's stipulation for a less active and direct US effort in military assistance, what is the future role of new technology for our tactical forces?

In the following pages, we shall propose that under the conditions likely to prevail in the future, the pursuit of advanced technology on a selective and imaginative basis affords the United States one of the best guarantees for maintaining international security. It is not always immediately obvious what the military payoffs of such technology may be. The estimates of cost-effectiveness will have to include many intangible factors. It is hardly possible, for example, to put a dollar value on the military significance of surveillance satellites, since their primary value is to lift a veil of ignorance. Yet neither the negotiations on limiting strategic arms nor the verification of compliance with arms agreements could be accomplished without satellite technology; indeed, this is a "technological fix" for the formerly insoluble political impasse regarding on-site inspection. Further, as our national experience with aircraft and solid state electronics (to cite only two instances) has demonstrated, great commercial and other benefits may occasionally be realized from areas of technology supported initially without a primary profit motive.

Before going into this subject, however, we shall outline our under-standing of some of the most important national and international trends likely to emerge in the years immediately ahead. We offer these conjectures not as an exhaustive review and certainly not as an authoritative statement, for we are not specialists in politics or for-eign policy. Rather, we wish to make clear some of the considerations upon which our recommendations about R&D are based.

2

Speculations on Future International Security

National Attitudes Toward National Security

The American people now appear to be committed to a major retrenchment of our foreign military commitments. These commitments were originally made during and after World War II, and were motivated primarily by considerations of self-defense coupled with an idealistic desire to preserve an open world wherever possible. The present mood of retrenchment seems to have wide popular support among the youth of the country, among many members of the Congress concerned with the past decade of war in Indochina and the next decade of competition in international trade, and among leaders of the intellectual community—not least, certain academicians who regard disarmament and military cutbacks as a moral crusade. The theme is widely supported in the news media. To be sure, there are some observers who still back the active internationalist tradition of the past 30 years, and who continue to favor selective military involvement abroad as part of what they consider to be a defensive strategy in behalf of the Free World. Yet both President Johnson and President Nixon have had to recognize the increasing opposition to this line of policy.

This debate is not new, of course. Our people have historically had mixed feelings about military intervention in external conflicts. George Washington's dictum on avoiding foreign entanglements is still regarded as the classic statement on the subject, although it should be remembered that he, too, sought French military aid during the Revolutionary War. Such a dualism also appears in the writings of Benjamin Franklin, who was perhaps our first statesman to give coherent thought to our national destiny. While supporting the westward expansion of our frontiers at the expense of other nations that had possessions in North America, he nevertheless hoped that the growing colonies would retain their cultural, linguistic, and ethnic homogeneity. Franklin ultimately became a strong advocate of revolution, once he concluded that the mother country—to which he was initially devoted—would never treat the people of the colonies on an equal footing with their cousins in Great Britain. At the same time, he worked closely with our revolutionary government to develop strong ties with France.

During the 19th century, we were aggressively imperialistic, but we limited our adventures mainly to practical territorial gains—extensions of the ever-present frontier. The culminating point of this phase of our national history was reached during the Spanish-American War, in which we acquired Puerto Rico and the Philippines.

The trend has been reversed in this century. Although we entered World War I on the side of the Allies, we demanded no indemnities or territorial compensations from our enemies, and signed a separate peace treaty with the defeated nations in the forthright spirit of "never again." Our involvement in World War II generated widespread popular support only after Pearl Harbor. We then accepted participation in the conflict both as a requirement of national security and as an inevitable mission in support of freedom and self-determination everywhere. It was assumed from the start, however, that we would not add to our territories as a result of the war, and that we would participate in the rehabilitation of the defeated as well as the victorious belligerents.

The zeal that involved us in world military affairs 30 years ago was sustained by the Cold War for about 15 years—through the war in Korea, and then in the creation of a broad network of alliances in Europe, the Near East, and Asia. But, partly as a result of new viewpoints expressed by the post-World War II generation, this zeal waned to the point where it could not be maintained through the conflict in Vietnam. Many people—indeed, many statesmen of the earlier era—have come to regard our military participation in troubled areas overseas as much too provocative, if not immoral. The Cold War is now seen as being transformed into a nonmilitary mode. Nationalism and militarism are judged as futile at best, and world war—unless triggered by some irrational act—is regarded as wildly improbable.

No aspirant for the Presidency can ignore this emerging attitude about the role of the United States in future patterns of international security. Unless an unusual event occurs to break the trend, it appears that our foreign involvements will decline over time and will become primarily political and economic in character, while our military posture will become more defensive and less oriented toward intervention, or even assistance, in foreign crises.

Some Speculations on Future Trends

If we assume that the United States will attempt to influence the world much less directly in the physical military sense during the coming period, it seems useful to try to forecast some of the consequences that might flow from this trend, and then suggest appropriate steps that should be taken to advance our national interests in the new framework.

Alternative US Moods. Two rather different trends could take hold in the next few years, following what we hope will be a durable resolution of the conflict in Southeast Asia.

In one case, the uproar of critical protest could continue to abate substantially, with the United States becoming much less involved in military commitments abroad while pursuing foreign policy objectives presumed to promote international harmony and economic development. If this trend prevails, the military aspects of national security policy could be discussed in an atmosphere of relative calm, with the widespread participation of many interest groups—as was true, for example, between 1945 and 1965. Even so, it would still be difficult to predict the outcome of such discussions, because the emotional atmosphere would be different from the period following World War II, when it was taken for granted that civilians had an obligation to cooperate in the constructive planning of all aspects of national defense.

Alternatively, our country might remain polarized by the recent debates on Vietnam long after the conflict subsides. Distrustful of the government and fearful of political conspiracies, many students and faculty in the universities, as well as other portions of the intellectual community, might remain staunchly antimilitary. In this scenario, concern for the military aspects of national security would be confined to specialized, full-time groups in the Departments of State and Defense, and in industrial and not-for-profit organizations.

We hope that the first of these possible moods will prevail, but we think it prudent to consider them both. Abstention from military involvement in any but the most grave foreign threats could lead to significant consequences, such as those we sketch next.

A Major External Threat Develops. In the most extreme—but not entirely implausible—situation, US military retrenchment could affect the prospects perceived by a military adventurer in a country such as the Soviet Union, a leader who might gamble that the time had come to attempt the conquest of a large part of the globe—for example, the entire Eurasian continent and its approaches.

To be sure, such an adventurer might emerge whatever the military policies of the United States. Indeed, there are those who argue that great US military strength, and a palpable willingness to employ it, make this scenario more rather than less likely, on the hypothesis that such a posture of preparedness stimulates Soviet militarism. In fact, however, Soviet restraint over the past quarter of a century in avoiding an all-out military confrontation with the United States seems to suggest the opposite—namely, that the Soviet Union is likely to move only where it enjoys overwhelming military superiority, as in Czechoslovakia in 1968. The caution of the Russian Politburo has been one of the major safeguards against the rise of a Soviet Napoleon thus far—this, plus the sentiment of the Soviet population at large, which has a deep-seated horror of war and would probably prefer to live-and-let-live with the Western world. Memories of the terrors of the Stalinist period have also played an important role in restraining the Soviet leadership from concentrating power too strongly in the hands of a single person.

Nevertheless, populations can be swayed by colorful and ambitious men, particularly as memories of the hardship of war recede; and a passive military posture on the part of the United States could turn out to be hazardous, especially if the same approach were not adopted by the other great powers, in particular the Soviet Union and Communist China. Some indication of the likelihood of this danger will be revealed by the spirit with which the Soviet Union accepts the limitations of the SALT Agreements. Will the Soviets arm to the absolute limit permitted by the first SALT accords? Or will Moscow now relax somewhat and settle for something less than the permissible limits in both strategic missiles and related naval capabilities? A comparable indicator will be the ultimate attitude of the Chinese toward such opportunities for detente as the nuclear Nonproliferation Treaty. China and the Soviet Union will also soon be faced with diplomatic and military choices affecting their relationships with Japan, and their actions will signal the capacity of the three nations to accommodate their competing interests in the Far East.

The vulnerability of a militarily relaxed United States to a massive surprise attack cannot be overstated. However repugnant such "unthinkable" events may be, a century that has witnessed two world wars and sometimes fierce ideological conflict must consider such a possibility. It is reasonable to ask what would happen if our available military capacity fell into the hands of what had become an ineffective and politicized military corps, lacking the confidence and will to react with sufficient speed to a global strategic threat launched by an aggressor having complete command over technologically advanced military forces. Such a danger would, of course, be heightened by continued divisiveness among the American people. Even in the absence of such an extreme external threat, the advocacy of extensive disarmament "hedged" with pledges to reconsider the defense budget in the event of a major crisis, ignores the lightning speed with which a future high-tension situation could escalate to major strategic war. As we briefly discuss later, unilateral restraint does not, in fact, seem to promote stability as much as negotiated restraints do.

Third World Conflicts Grow. A second scenario involves the rise of mini-Caesars in several smaller countries. Militaristic "liberators" might take it upon themselves to alter borders and overthrow neighboring governments as circumstances permit, and they might feel much freer to act if the United States continuously reduced its military presence overseas.

In the past quarter of a century, such leaders have often been encouraged by the moral and material support of the Communist Bloc countries. During a period when the United States was cutting back its military commitments, international stability would largely depend upon whether other major nations supported or restrained adventurers. If the Soviet Union and Communist China continue to provide support for "wars of national liberation," there may be more frequent aggressions such as those of North Korea and North Vietnam, with a consequent shrinkage of the Free World. This scenario could unfold quickly and evolve in ways hard to brake and reverse.

International Recriminations Increase. There is at least a third important possibility: a violent upheaval of American opinion, accompanied by a frenetic search for individuals and groups upon whom to fix "blame" for the decline of our worldwide political and military strength.

At present, the voices encouraging withdrawal from foreign involvements, including a military presence when needed, are quite widespread. But if ever the public should decide that all this was in error, and that it was a tragic mistake to reduce our military strength and worldwide strategic posture, there could be a violent reaction—perhaps comparable to the McCarthy era, when the admiration for the Soviet Union which had developed during World War II turned to fear and led to a search for traitors. McCarthyism failed not only because events soon demonstrated that we were still enormously strong relative to the Soviet Union, but also because McCarthy himself was exposed on national television as an outrageous demagogue.

For example, should our withdrawal from Vietnam be followed by a North Vietnamese takeover of the South, and should neighboring governments collapse under conditions that gave rise to widespread concern about our ability to control events, the public reaction could be bitter. Similarly, increasing Soviet power in the Mediterranean could heighten our difficulties in dealing with the Arab oil-exporting countries. Should this occur as our energy problems worsened, the public would ask whether our new strategic weakness makes sense, and whether the apparent military savings had become too costly.

These three brief and incomplete scenarios—the emergence of a major foreign threat, the proliferation of minor conflicts and conquests in the Third World incompatible with US interests, and a sudden turnaround in US opinion as to what our foreign policies should be—suggest only a few of the variations of trends that could develop. They clearly show the need for moderation in the rate at which we revise our foreign policies.

Alternative Approaches for US Policy

In considering the current retrenchment of US foreign policy and the potential hazards it offers to national and international security, what can be done to minimize the dangers?

We will not be concerned here with nonmilitary foreign aid programs—which we believe should be expanded, not contracted—because such programs do not relate directly to the role of military

R&D in international security affairs. Nor will we be concerned with US participation in the agencies of the United Nations—although here, too, we believe there is ample justification for increased participation by the United States and, particularly, by our scientists and technologists.

Effective international policies will depend, of course, upon the degree to which we can regain unity of purpose at home, the elusive "high morale" that derives from a consensus on national objectives. The restoration of such unity is probably the most important, and difficult, immediate goal. Nor can we be sure that we shall achieve it. The free nations of Western Europe did not succeed in rising adequately to the evident challenge they faced in the 1930s prior to the outbreak of war. Indeed, a period of disunity in the face of uncertainty seems to be an inescapable characteristic of the democratic system, especially when the issues under dispute take on a moralistic tone arousing crosscurrents of passion similar to religious conflict.

Negotiations. One of the alternatives open to us is to place even greater reliance upon international negotiations such as the Strategic Arms Limitation Talks—which led to the May 1972 Agreements with the Soviet Union—and the new, highly promising relationship with Communist China. Our national interest—our stake in international security—mandates the goal of peaceful coexistence, and no one will deny the attractiveness of serious negotiations in achieving this goal. The world simply must try harder to live in harmony. In the long run, there is no satisfactory alternative. In the short run, the beginning of a process of institutionalized negotiations on the most sensitive issues is the great contribution of SALT.

But the success of this effort clearly depends upon the general acceptance of genuinely peaceful coexistence—in practice as well as in principle—by all of the major powers, which would be expected, in turn, to use their influence to this end on the smaller countries. The benchmark of success, the end-point of negotiations, would be a pattern of international relationships characterized by the worldwide exercise of restraint and by an enduring process of accommodation. This is a demanding goal.

For example, would the Soviet Union be willing to negotiate seriously with the Chinese on the degree of real independence to be accorded to Outer Mongolia? Would both Chinese and Soviet leaders be prepared to restrain North Korea if Pyongyang again exhibited a desire to overthrow the South Korean government? Would the United States be willing to provide substantial economic aid to the Communist government of Cuba, provided Cuba would forego further support or participation in Communist revolutionary activity elsewhere in Latin America? Can the chaotic situation in the Middle East be transformed into a stable settlement, or will the Soviet Union be tempted to use its expanding naval force in the Mediterranean as a basis for aggressive political purposes? It is not easy to visualize these situations being resolved wholly independently of military considerations.

All of this assumes, further, that the major nuclear powers would live up to generalized SALT-like agreements ultimately covering all important forms of armament and military preparedness, and that they would not attempt to deceive the system. We believe that the success of such comprehensive arms controls will ultimately require the acceptance of a much higher measure of reciprocal surveillance or trust than seems possible today, especially where agreements might limit qualitative, technological improvements in existing systems. Perhaps the single most important goal is to win time, so that the will to negotiate our differences will have a chance eventually to emerge. But such a development, however devoutly we may wish for it, will be much less likely if an ambitious leader of one of the closed societies sees an opportunity to achieve easy victory through aggression and threat rather than through negotiation and compromise.

Simplistic theories about bargaining chips in negotiations, like simplistic notions of military-industrial conspiracies, are not valid. But it is also true that the United States tends to negotiate internally and in public and then to concede perhaps too much before bilateral negotiations begin. The history of our ABM program and the Soviet reactions to it, before and during SALT I, as well as the history of our advanced submarine-missile program and the Soviet willingness to include some interim limits on submarines during SALT I, suggest that we must be prepared to pursue our own goals in our own interests until we can achieve satisfactory, reciprocal limitations. To the degree that this line of thinking is sound, it means that defense R&D must provide a range of clearly defined options but must *not* be allowed to produce an independent momentum toward procurement of advanced systems that could destabilize past or prospective arms agreements.

Alliances A second route in the search for security (and one not necessarily excluded by an emphasis on superpower negotiations) is to encourage the development of various alliance systems that would ultimately interact to produce a viable, multipolar balance of power.

For example, the present Administration in Washington seems to hope that the European Economic Community may form an independent military unit without the United States, and by itself safeguard the approaches to Western Europe, including the Mediterranean. In effect, the countries of Western Europe would take over the structures of NATO as their own and leave the United States to pursue a more detached but still basically friendly course toward them, as was true before World War II. Can Western Europe, in view of its long history of internal rivalry and conflict, achieve the necessary will and sense of unity to implement such a policy consistently and persistently in the coming decade or two? Would the Soviet Union long tolerate a free-standing, adequately armed Western Europe on the borders of its empire? Soviet acceptance of NATO has presumably derived largely from its reluctance to challenge the United States. The imminent negotiations on mutual and balanced force reductions may well provide a crucial indicator of the feasibility of a West European alliance independent of the United States.

The difficulties confronting the establishment of an independent defensive federation in Western Europe would be amplified manyfold if any attempt were made to encourage such a federation in the Western Pacific. There, Japanese leadership would be central. But quite apart from the apparently deep Japanese aversion to large-scale rearmament and especially to nuclear weapons, other Asian nations would fear a remilitarized Japan with its enormous industrial and technical strength; and some might even turn to the

Communist countries for a measure of reassurance. In light of their history of rivalry and their presently low industrial capacity, it is even less likely that the nations around the Indian Ocean could form an effective, independent defensive alliance.

It might be argued that our proper position in the world would be to encourage the rivalry of potential antagonists, and to attempt to establish for ourselves the leverage for delicately balancing a global power system. This would involve the encouragement of distrust between mainland China and the Soviet Union. But with the profound antagonisms that still seem to obsess the Communist superpowers, such a policy would be explosively dangerous. It might stimulate an arms race that could easily get out of hand, as occurred in Europe prior to World War I, and lead to the worldwide conflict it was designed to forestall.

Moderate Retrenchment with Preparedness It appears, therefore, that the most effective means of increasing stability in the world is for the United States to maintain considerable military strength, both to deter strategic conflict and to minimize the potential for major wars in the developing countries, while participating energetically in international negotiations aimed at reliable arms control and disarmament. At the same time, the United States should move to reduce minor military commitments abroad, to disengage at a measured pace, where circumstances permit, in order to repair the fabric of domestic unity torn apart by the Vietnam conflict. At the risk of oversimplification, we call this framework Moderate Retrenchment with Preparedness. Its benefit lies in its realistic recognition of the contemporary domestic and international conditions within which foreign policy must function. It is not an inspired policy, of course, because it merely codifies the trend of the past few years. But we hope that by focusing squarely on its main features, it will be possible to establish the minimum safe level of retrenchment and then to think through our other related actions more coherently.

We recognize that a policy of military retrenchment may cause friendly nations to doubt whether we would be willing to assist them in the event of trouble. But we think this price must be paid if the national consensus on foreign policy is to be restored. Meanwhile, we would maintain strong bilateral and multilateral links with our friends throughout the world and vigorously encourage international negotiations on a variety of fronts.

Moreover, we emphasize that moderate retrenchment must be accompanied by the maintenance of a strong strategic preparedness program coupled to a flexible tactical capability. The United States will not contribute its full share to the maintenance of international peace and security unless we possess a powerful military capability that is both credible and diversified. To be credible, a military capability must demonstrate competence at all levels, not least in terms of advanced technology. To be diversified, it must be effective both defensively and offensively, tactically and strategically. To avoid tempting others into military aggression, our capability must be neither muscle-bound nor provocative. The size of our forces will be limited by financial constraints and by international conditions and agreements. But today, size is less important than effectiveness; quality and ingenuity must take priority over mere numbers. So we turn now to our main subject: the research and development that can provide this quality and ingenuity for much of the operation and equipment of our forces.

3

Strengthening R&D in the Interest of
International Security, Part One

Research and development are needed to sustain military preparedness in the face of the present trend toward military retrenchment. Ideally, a new program along the lines we advocate would
merit and should receive the cooperation of a number of civilian
groups in our nation. If left primarily to military planners, the end
result probably would not be optimum. It is not that the professional
military staff lacks imagination or ready access to some sources of
technical skill. Rather, the military staff tends to be imprisoned by
traditions emphasizing discipline, responsibility toward rank, and
numbers of standing forces equipped with established gear. In the
formative stages of a new policy, we need wide-ranging and flexible
attitudes, not to speak of certain changes in the R&D program.

What are the steps that should be taken to acquire the technological strength needed to stabilize international security? In view

of our own participation in defense R&D programs, the authors are probably more sympathetic than some would be to the needs and strengths of defense R&D. We are also keenly aware of the mistakes, problems, and criticisms of defense R&D. What follows is our attempt to formulate a few of the main principles of a plan for defense R&D that is in the national interest: a plan designed to build, not erode, international security. It is offered neither as an ideal formula nor as a new doctrine, but as a preliminary case for debate.

To be most effective, we believe defense R&D requires more vigorous action in at least five major areas.

Strategic Planning. We need broader and more imaginative planning studies centered on national security, involving as wide a range of our citizens as possible and following the pattern of debate and broad participation by the many creative professionals who were so effective in the period between 1945 and 1965. The new strategic issues of deterrence and stability raised by conditions of US-Soviet parity, together with the related budgetary choices, need to be assessed more deeply. These studies should coherently integrate topics such as the next major arms control steps, and the possible development and deployment of new weapons intended to deter or neutralize real strategic threats. Flexibility would be emphasized because, as we have urged, vigorous international negotiations on disarmament would also be going on. Finally, it is very important that secrecy be radically reduced. Secrecy hinders progress in policy analysis, in R&D itself, and in public appreciation of our alternatives.

Tactical Needs. We also require imaginative new approaches to the problems of tactical warfare that were downgraded between 1945 and 1960 because of high-level decisions, justifiable at the time, to place primary emphasis on strategic issues and systems. This area of work would interact strongly with the first; tactical planning must focus on the overall policy implications of the Nixon Doctrine as applied to our worldwide commitments in whatever form they take. Great attention must be given to low-cost, high-reliability, multipurpose tactical technologies that fulfill our apparently changing requirements.

Technology Base. This means the encouragement, on a selective basis, of all technologies which could have a bearing on our own long-range capability and enhance our understanding of the military potential of other nations. Many of these fields would have relevance for both military and civilian applications—such as computer technology, which will continue to have commercial importance in the future. But defense R&D must also relate to technologies that show long-range, but still uncertain, promise for either military or other purposes.

Prototypes. The design and construction of a limited number of prototype systems, tested thoroughly to provide the technical innovations pertinent to decisions about defensive and offensive capabilities, are also necessary. More work with such prototypes would allow us to assess the capabilities of other nations potentially able to threaten international peace. Equally important, fully implemented prototype analysis would lead to greater economy and less risk in any required production runs.

Testing. Finally, fresh and more searching methods for the testing and evaluation of new systems are essential. Traditionally, testing the effectiveness of a new defense system has been the responsibility of the procuring government agency, cooperating closely with the contractor designing and manufacturing the system. Although the Defense Department's R&D leaders have recently been expanding departmental testing programs, a study should be made of techniques to ensure more thorough and more independent evaluations carried out in as objectively neutral an environment as possible.

The overall R&D program envisioned here might cost more in the next few years, as some new efforts are started while certain major programs already under way are concluded. We recommend greater emphasis on exploratory work and less emphasis on development, assuming this can be justified in terms of the international situation. Projecting further arms control agreements, we also anticipate a long-range reduction in overall defense R&D funding. The immediate—and long-run—aim is to increase confidence in the nation's overall technological position as related to international security.

As an introduction to the discussion of these five specific areas, it may be helpful to review contemporary trends in the funding of defense R&D.

Patterns of Defense R&D, 1953-1972

Because of the great interest in—and, unfortunately, considerable misunderstanding of—the role of defense R&D within the country's overall technological base, we have included as an appendix to this monograph a lengthy excerpt from *The Economics of Defense Spending: A Look at the Realities,* a 1972 compilation of facts and arguments on the impact of the Department of Defense upon technology and industry. Prepared by the Comptroller of the Department of Defense and presented in summary form to the Congress, the compilation is a lively, official contribution to current policy debates. It contains critical data that are scarcely appreciated by some observers. Let us review some highlights of the data.

To begin with, consider the frequently made charge that "defense R&D has dominated federal—and national—R&D funding since the post-World War II years." This is certainly no longer true. The following data from the National Science Foundation show the trends clearly.

Table 1

Sources of US R&D Funds by Sector
($ billions)

	1953	1958	1963	1968	1972 (Est.)
Federal Government:					
Defense-related	$2.5	$ 5.7	$ 7.1	$ 8.5	$ 8.1
Space-related	–	.1	2.4	3.3	2.9
All other	.2	1.0	1.8	3.1	4.2
Total, Federal Government	$2.8	$ 6.8	$11.2	$15.0	$15.2

Non-Federal Government

Industry	$2.2	$ 3.7	$ 5.4	$ 9.0	$11.3
Universities and colleges	.2	.3	.5	.8	1.1
Other nonprofit institutions	.1	.1	.2	.3	.4
Total, Non-Federal Government	$2.5	$ 4.1	$ 6.1	$10.1	$12.8

Summaries:

Defense-related	$2.5	$ 5.7	$ 7.1	$ 8.5	$ 8.1
All other	2.7	5.2	10.3	16.6	19.9
Total, US R&D	$5.2	$10.9	$17.4	$25.1	$28.0

Source: National Science Foundation, *National Patterns of R&D Resources, 1953-1972.* NSF 72-300, December 1971, pp. 32 and 34. Adapted from *The Economics of Defense Spending: A Look at the Realities.*

It is also interesting to review the trends in terms of percentage shares. Table 2 makes it difficult to conclude that other R&D efforts have been starved for funds in order to make room for defense projects.

Table 2

Percent of Total US R&D Effort

	1953	1958	1963	1968	1972
Defense-related	47.5%	52.0%	40.6%	33.9%	29.0%
Space-related	.8	1.0	13.7	13.2	10.4
Subtotal	48.3	53.0	54.3	47.1	39.4
All other	51.7	47.0	45.7	52.9	60.6
Total	100.0	100.0	100.0	100.0	100.0

Source: National Patterns of R&D Resources, 1953-1972, p. 34. See also the Appendix.

An even more revealing way to examine the trends is in terms of constant prices, and these data are shown in Table 3. Very few observers are aware that defense R&D in 1972, in constant prices, was at a level *below* the level of 1958. All of the real growth in the R&D resources of the United States since 1958—more than $8 billion—has been applied to civilian activities. Furthermore, total

R&D constant-price funding dropped seven percent between 1968 and 1972—an unfortunate trend—while both defense and space R&D were being curtailed. This suggests that there was no pent-up readiness to invest heavily in civilian R&D.

Table 3

Summary of US R&D Funds by Sector
(In billions of CY 1958 dollars)

			Calendar Years		
	1953	*1958*	*1963*	*1968*	*1972 (Est.)*
Federal Government:					
Defense-related	$2.8	$5.7	$6.6	$7.0	$5.5
Space-related	–	.1	2.2	2.7	2.0
All other	.3	1.0	1.7	2.6	2.8
Total, Federal Government	3.1	6.8	10.5	12.3	10.4
Non-Federal:					
Industry	2.5	3.7	5.1	7.4	7.7
Universities and colleges	.2	.3	.5	.7	.7
Other nonprofit institutions	.1	.1	.2	.3	.3
Total, Non-Federal Government	2.8	4.1	5.7	8.3	8.7
Summaries:					
Defense-related	2.8	5.7	6.6	7.0	5.5
All other	3.1	5.2	9.6	13.6	13.5
Total, US R&D	5.9	10.9	16.2	20.6	19.1

Source: Table 1, deflated with GNP deflator, taken from Appendix. The National Science Foundation also uses GNP deflator for stating totals in constant prices (*see National Patterns of R&D Resources, 1953-1972*, p. 2), but uses a CY 1967 base. The CY 1958 base is used for consistency with other data. Use of a different base year does not alter relationships among the years. Rounded figures may not add to rounded totals.

Having reviewed the broad trends in spending, let us now consider a few other, more specific points of criticism about defense R&D. For example, some critics of defense R&D have said that "the Defense Department dominates university research." This has not been true for at least 15 years, and it is certainly not true today, as the data in Table 4 reveal. In fact, the defense share of total national support to academic R&D dropped from 25 percent of the total in 1956 to eight percent in 1972. (We are excluding here the special nonprofit centers associated with some universities, but the trends are comparable and data on these activities are given in the Appendix.) Even the defense share of total Federal support dropped from 57 percent in 1956 to 14 percent in 1972. We might ask whether this is enough support, rather than too much.

Table 4

*Sources of Funds for R&D Performed in Colleges
and Universities*
($ millions)

	1956	1961	1964	1968	1972
R&D Performed in Colleges and Universities					
Federal Government:					
Defense	$122	$198	$ 295	$ 307	$ 246
Space	1	15	90	138	105
All other programs	90	287	531	1,127	1,399
Total, Federal Government	213	500	916	1,572	1,750
Industry	29	40	41	55	65
Universities, colleges, and state and local governments	204	371	555	841	1,060
Other nonprofit institutions	34	58	83	131	175
Total	480	969	1,595	2,599	3,050
Defense as percent of:					
Federal funding	57.3%	39.6%	32.2%	19.5%	14.1%
Total R&D at colleges & universities	25.4%	20.4%	18.5%	11.8%	8.1%

Source: *National Patterns of R&D Resources, 1953-1972.* See also the Appendix.

Another specific issue that has often been raised about defense R&D concerns the priorities on national manpower. Is defense

R&D monopolizing the country's trained scientists and engineers? The answer is, Not today, and not during the past decade. Table 5 gives data on this matter.

Table 5

Full-Time Equivalent Scientists and Engineers Employed in R&D (in thousands)

		Approximate Breakdown	
	Total	*Defense-Related*	*All Other*
1954	236.8	114.1	122.7
1958	354.7	184.4	170.3
1961	425.2	209.2	216.0
1965	496.5	160.4	336.1
1968	550.6	186.6	364.0
1969	559.4	188.0	371.4
1970	544.6	159.0	385.6
1971	519.4	149.1	370.3

Source: *National Patterns of R&D Resources, 1953-1972.* See also the Appendix.

Unfortunately, the total national scientific and engineering employment has been declining. But it is hard to conclude from the overall trend that defense work has been a major factor in "diverting" R&D capabilities from other pressing tasks.

Let us consider one additional point, namely, whether the large Department of Defense budget has so pervasively influenced private industry that technical innovation in civilian fields has been blocked. First, keep in mind that about half of the Department's budget pays the wages and salaries of military and civilian employees, who buy the same range of consumer goods that all of us do. Now, if we set aside aircraft and ordnance—of which Defense understandably purchases over half the total national production—the Department buys, with all of the rest of its budget, about 2.5 percent of the total national output of goods and services. It is hard to believe that this share could somehow dominate the pattern of the other 97.5 percent of buyers and sellers.

We do not note these facts in order to justify unlimited or even increased budgets for the Defense Department. Indeed, in this essay and elsewhere, the authors have argued for greater economy in many segments of the defense program. However, in assessing the case for defense R&D, there is no point in bringing up straw men and irrelevant or misleading cause-effect relationships, as some observers have done. The debate must focus on national goals for R&D that serve our foreign and military policies and have the objective of stabilizing the international situation. With this in mind, we will forego further consideration of budgets and move on to the five broad R&D areas that seem to us to require more emphasis in the next few years. Two of these will be considered in the balance of this chapter, and the other three in the next chapter.

Planning and Analysis of Strategic Options

Prior to 1940, problems of national security, and particularly the related technical problems, were analyzed only by the military agencies. It is true that during World War I there was some civilian participation through organizations such as the National Research Council, but this had largely disappeared by the time the international crises of the 1930s emerged.

The situation changed radically early in World War II with the creation of the Office of Scientific Research and Development and the Manhattan District—both operating under the direction of distinguished scientist-statesmen with the blessings of the White House. These organizations brought a large number of civilians from other walks of life into close association with the problems of national security at both the strategic and tactical levels. Our nation benefited enormously from this participation, since the work of these groups accelerated the development and use of such systems as radar and antisubmarine devices, thereby shortening the war and saving lives.

At first, many professional military leaders resented their relatively unorthodox colleagues and resisted cooperation with them. The civilian scientists tended to use methods of debate and discussion which resembled the academic seminar rather than the military briefing. But the attitude of the military staffs changed as the war progressed. They found that they had much to gain through coopera- tion. By the end of World War II, most military leaders were eager to retain the cooperation of nongovernmental civilians, and, in fact, took pride in such associations. Advisory committees of many types were created. *Ad hoc* groups were formed to study almost all major issues and many minor ones. Institutions separate from government yet linked to the government's policymaking process—such as RAND and Lincoln Laboratory—were created to provide detailed analysis of problems on a continuing basis.

Almost every agency of the government was exposed to advice from members of the intellectual community, especially from the scientists. Later, the President decided to establish his own Science Advisor, who was, in turn, provided with an advisory committee. The Joint Chiefs of Staff encouraged the formation of the in-house Weapons System Evaluation Group as well as an independent but closely associated nonprofit organization, the Institute for Defense Analyses (IDA). Originally placed under the management of a group of universities in order to bring together dedicated analysts from diverse academic areas, IDA was especially close to the problems of the Joint Chiefs of Staff. Secretary McNamara perhaps crowned this evolution by developing an academically-oriented in-house civilian group—under the Assistant Secretary of Defense for Sys- tems Analysis—to carry out cost-feasibility studies on many military choices by using the techniques of operational and systems analysis. This trend, which extended unbroken until the mid-1960s, was highly productive on many frontiers and, in an important sense, represented the ideal collaboration of the interested, independent professional citizen with his government.

One obligation assumed by both the part-time advisors and the full-time but short-term (two to five years) senior staff drawn from the academic and industrial R&D community was a measure of confidentiality about the policies debated. Until the last few years, civilians invited to participate in the national advisory structure were meticulous in observing the confidential nature of their associa- tions. Debate about the war in Vietnam changed this. Conflicts grew so bitter and were so often framed in moral terms that some past advisors became unwilling to serve further. Recruitment of civilians into senior positions in the Defense Department became more difficult, and many advisors and employees were prepared—or felt compelled—to violate the confidential agreements they had made. Indeed, the mixed feelings about the Ellsberg case symbolize a new chapter in this relationship of intellectuals to the government's national security organizations, and could cast a long shadow into the future.

Our country would gain immeasurably if the intellectual community, including its younger members, would again join in cooperative working relations with the government, lending strength and imagination to improving the ongoing system, and looking upon the problems of national security as part of the goal of preserving freedom and building stable international security arrangements. To do this effectively, the participants will probably have to recognize that the pursuit of arms control—critically essential for survival now as well as in the future—may require upgrading of our military technology to assure that our defensive system has credibility during the periods of negotiation that lie ahead. At the time this monograph is written, however, the suggestion that one work inside the system is anathema to many individuals who would have sought (or at least accepted) such participation a decade or more ago. This is a major problem of our time.

It is a twofold problem. The nation loses the breadth and depth of insights that might sharpen the goals, tighten the management, and reduce the costs of defense R&D. And the nation does not replenish its diminishing resources of experienced civilians who, during and after their services as senior advisors or staff employees, independently debate and constructively criticize those international security choices that are entangled with critical scientific issues.

In the foreseeable future, our academic centers may not provide much help to the Department of Defense. In this connection, however, we should recall that at no time in recent history have universities in Europe or Asia engaged in serious in-depth studies of national security, as was the case in the United States between 1940 and 1965. That quarter of a century may come to be regarded as unique. We may have to depend more upon free-standing institutions which are outside, but have some of the spirit of, the academic world as centers for those who wish to work in an official advisory capacity on military matters.

One great obstacle to the reestablishment of cooperation between the military and academic civilian communities is the deep distrust that has grown up. Scarred by the debates about Vietnam and scorched again by the Watergate affair, government officials and scientist-advisors have exchanged charges of irrationality, irresponsibility, and political expediency too often for them to be soon forgotten. Dramatic new events and an entirely new generation may be needed to change these attitudes.

We have dwelt on the people and the atmosphere involved in our strategic planning because it is essential that serious and wide-ranging studies be organized, and that the professionally most competent analysts of all ages and inclinations meet regularly with those having full-time responsibility for national security. How can this be promoted? We believe that there are two specific opportunities for making significant progress.

First, *secrecy* must be—and can be—greatly reduced so that the main features of the technical choices affecting defense policy will be better known to both the general public and the scientific and engineering community. In general, secrecy in R&D should be applied only in the final stages of the development process, when equipment is headed for production and, in effect, is part of the general inventory. With much less secrecy about R&D efforts and about the strategic problems and policies being evaluated, university advisors would be more likely to participate in study groups. With less secrecy surrounding the conclusions of studies, the public and the Congress would better understand the policy alternatives and would debate these choices more coherently. Finally, the effectiveness of most laboratories engaged in defense R&D would increase significantly if there were fewer constraints on the traditional and powerful processes of critical review among specialists. In short, less secrecy would stimulate many more talented scientists and engineers to recognize the serious issues at stake.

Second, a few clear-cut issues must be shown to be sufficiently challenging to deserve special attention. In particular, we believe that future planning involving R&D must focus sharply on two strategic concepts—*sufficiency* and *parity*—that are central to the nation's security. In the past, the United States had unmistakable leads in strategic technology and strategic forces. Today, those leads are largely gone. Now the strategic forces of the United States and the Soviet Union are roughly equal, at parity. Thus, theories based upon US superiority are presumably no longer valid. Now we apparently are aiming for sufficient forces to provide a stable deterrent, that is, for conditions that promote increasingly reliable arms control and a lowered probability of nuclear war between the superpowers. But sufficiency is very hard to define or measure precisely. As with safety precautions, each observer answers the question, "How much is enough?" in a different way. We also know that stability is a fragile feature of the international environment, and that it includes many psychological as well as physical components. In short, many current debates about arms control are still organized in terms of a vague mixture of old "superiority" theories and current "parity" realities.

Consider, for example, the following questions. Instead of the classic triad of bombers plus land-based and sea-based missiles, would the least vulnerable component, the submarine force, be sufficient? If so, should it be improved to ensure against the possibility of Soviet countermeasures? What new indications of Soviet intentions have been emerging from the talks on limiting strategic arms? Are there new steps that should be taken to strengthen deterrence without being provocative? Without in any way implying that Washington does not have these questions in mind, the authors believe that the nation needs more *independent* work on such issues and the related national policies. For without a higher degree of consensus on a sound conceptual basis for our current and future military policies, Congressional reviews of the R&D budgets related to the *next generation* of systems will continue to be buffeted wildly by lobbyists on all sides of key questions, and in consequence, we may drift into costly mistakes.

In short, actions to achieve assured sufficiency and a stable parity may be quite different from actions that were required to fulfill past national goals. Fresh technological thinking is needed. Thus, we must construct a new strategic framework and explore the needs for R&D within the new framework. These issues are important enough to involve the country's best analysts.

Reassessment of Tactical Needs

In the period following World War II, it was evident that a vast revolution in strategic warfare had been started by the development of nuclear explosives and large rocket motors. As a result, many of our military leaders, particularly those in the Air Force, focused almost entirely on the development of strategic weapons, and gave only secondary emphasis to tactical warfare. This tendency continued even during the Korean War, when the Army devoted substantial attention at the research and development level to such items as the gun-fired nuclear shell and the liquid-fueled rocket, and was inclined to use World War II ordnance in relatively unchanged form.

This pattern persisted during the 1950s, in spite of the lessons learned in Korea and the growing evidence of insurgency based on guerrilla tactics throughout Southeast Asia. We entered the Vietnamese conflict unprepared, both physically and psychologically, for the type of tactical situations we were to experience. Although it is much too complex a question to discuss in detail here, one wonders, for example, whether it would have been possible to achieve dramatically better results in Vietnam by depending exclusively upon a smaller force of specially equipped and trained units such as the Special Forces, instead of relying on large numbers of conventional troops.

In defense of military planners, the greatest and most apparent military threat to our national security since 1945 has been from strategic nuclear weapons. If a choice had to be made, such weapons deserved the highest attention and priority in procurement. Yet it remains unclear why the services, particularly the Army, did not exhibit far more interest in tactical warfare and in innovative tactical technology.

A most conspicuous example of this shortsightedness, which has received a great deal of attention, are the highly accurate, socalled "smart bombs" which were available (albeit in small numbers) in 1967 when we were bombing North Vietnamese targets, but which were not utilized extensively until 1971-72. It is even more significant that the United States command in Southeast Asia made so little use of sophisticated civilian advisors—including the few social scientists who had studied the country and the operations analysts who had assessed the actual effectiveness of our units. Unfortunately, even though the experience of World War II had amply demonstrated how useful civilan advisors could be, planning and evaluation were carried out largely by military staff.

Depending upon what definitions are used, our tactical forces—the "general purpose" forces, as they are called officially—cost $50-60 billion annually and involve most of the 2.3 million men and women in uniform. The size, character, disposition, and technological caliber of these forces relate to our own security and to the security of our allies. Yet informed observers generally, and the R&D community in particular, have been notably uninterested in the policies guiding this large national program spanning hundreds of projects and bases. Recently, criticism has grown concerning individual tactical aircraft now in development, such as the F-14 and F-15, certain long-stalled efforts such as the Army's new tank, and major interservice rivalries such as those influencing the requirements for new helicopters. This criticism has highlighted the large investments we are making and the arbitrariness of some of the programs.

But these debates go on because there is still no broad rationale for the size and needs of our forces, a rationale that takes account of both continuing and new US goals. Analysts debate the merits of a new "one-and-a-half war" policy versus the old "two-and-a-half war" policy; but few citizens even recognize this jargon, let alone understand it. And there is still no soundly based and firmly administered effort to modernize our forces for whatever new roles they will be asked to carry out in the post-Vietnam period.

Modernization is more than just a vague goal. A new and potentially overriding reason for carrying out R&D designed to assist our tactical program is the severe economic pressure arising from the greatly increased pay scales for the new all-volunteer military forces. Leaving aside the issue of whether an all-volunteer force is a sound concept in social and political terms—and we do not think it is, because it further divorces the professional military from continuous contacts with a broad cross section of the population—its financial impact has already been enormous. The new bonuses and higher pay scales will probably lead to even greater restrictions on total manpower in the armed forces. Thus research and development must be counted upon to maximize the efficiency of both the tools and the operating systems of our limited forces.

Compounding all of these technical and planning gaps is the deeper problem that, although the theory of graduated escalation applied in Vietnam was mostly a product of civilian political decisions in Washington, the apparent military failures in Vietnam will haunt us for a long while. Indeed, the country's present bitter divisiveness and discontent about all things military will probably persist while the services try to take a new hard look at their approach to the tactical forces.

In spite of what we may regard as our best intentions, international incidents requiring nonnuclear tactical action could occur under conditions we could not ignore. To meet this need, the known technological problems associated with tactical warfare deserve much higher priority. In addition, new R&D requirements may be identified as the present ambiguities about fulfilling the Nixon Doctrine with a smaller and much more highly paid volunteer force are resolved. Overall, the underlying uncertainties about what areas and levels of R&D would be responsive to our potential tactical commitments are quite comparable to those we have already mentioned in connection with the concept of strategic sufficiency.

4

Strengthening R&D in the Interest of International Security, Part Two

Selective Investment in Critical Technologies

This brings us to what is probably the most important theme in our discussion: the desirability, as we see it, of maintaining national technological leadership in as many areas as we can. There are many reasons in favor of this policy and many benefits to be gained from it, and most of them bear on national security. Let us outline the broad framework.

To begin with, it is worth emphasizing that there are three main purposes for exploring a given field of technology. First, to pursue normal commercial markets. Second, to advance general national needs—such as education, transportation, housing, health, defense, and, occasionally, national prestige. Third, to seize opportunities for new knowledge—advancing science and technology on their own terms, so to speak. Characteristically, because of the interplay among fields of science and engineering, efforts aimed at one of these purposes often produce progress toward one or more of the others. Such consequences are usually unpredictable.

The natural forces working to promote economic advance—largely, but not entirely, found in private industry—engender technological innovations having commercial interest. But when profit margins are under pressure, there is a tendency for industrial organizations to cut the most long-range research and development—which might have the most revolutionary effects—in order to bolster short-range profits. However, there now seems to be a renewed understanding by our senior governmental officials that our foreign trade depends upon the strength of industrial research and development in the most advanced fields of technology. We hope that this sharpened understanding will lead to increased governmental sponsorship of such research, either by direct grants or by special tax relief for private investment in industrial R&D. At the present time, the Department of Commerce and the National Science Foundation are in the early stages of grappling with this goal through various institutional experiments and programs for testing new incentives to induce more widespread, commercially successful innovations. Some of these experiments might help defense R&D by increasing the number of companies capable of conceiving and competing for high-technology projects.

Technical innovations are determined primarily by the general health of science and, especially, of the experimental sciences. It is not widely appreciated that many important fields of technology—such as those concerned with high-vacuum equipment, X-ray therapy, structural analysis, and microwave devices—originated as auxiliaries to the pursuit of pure science. While the needs of scientists for specialized equipment often run far ahead of the interests or capabilities of industry, the flow is by no means only in one direction. Advances in industrially-generated equipment or techniques may open doorways for the pursuit of science by providing new tools. For example, the general-purpose computers designed for the commercial market are also widely used for scientific work. Incidentally, development of these computers was stimulated initially by defense needs. As another illustration, the industrial development of plastics has provided scientists with a wide range of new materials used in the experimental equipment making possible new lines of study.

There are a number of fields of science and technology which either are so expensive or have potential end-uses which lie so far in the future that it is not possible to justify pursuing them in a strictly short-range, cost-effective sense through public or private funding. Much of the work of the National Aeronautics and Space Agency and the National Institute of Health falls into this category. Nevertheless, it is highly important that such work be undertaken as a truly national investment of public funds. The resulting technology may have important long-range impact on the missions to which it was originally intended to contribute, and ultimately on a much wider domain. In some cases, such as the first earth satellites and the Apollo program, the immediate result may be the enhancement of national prestige; and only later do other payoffs clearly emerge, such as weather forecasting and geophysical exploration. In other cases, such as the ill-fated supersonic transport, the endeavor may have been designed to provide insurance against losing leadership in a field from which we have derived large benefits.

The proposed space shuttle provides an example of one of the costly items of technological advance that could have an important bearing on our long-range national technical capability. It has no immediately needed military applications, and its impact on the economy is highly unpredictable. Although the space shuttle could prove to be very useful for astronomical research outside the atmosphere, the cost of a prototype could not be justified on that basis alone during this period when expenditures for basic science are being restricted.

Projects such as the space shuttle should be nurtured at a reasoned pace partly because they lie in areas contiguous to those in which we have considerable national competence and from which we have already gained much, both commercially and in relation to national security. In one sense, these projects are evolutionary steps beyond well-known frontiers. Yet they also open completely new vistas, and we are not yet in a position to grasp the full implications of these opportunities for the national future.

One of the arguments commonly given against this view is that the funds could be used instead for alleviating poverty or promoting public health, fields which are not being neglected but surely could be pushed more vigorously. While this legitimate viewpoint cannot be dismissed, the preservation of the broad technological capabilities upon which our national security rests is also a great public goal and warrants sustained emphasis. Wise trade-offs of this kind are never easy to strike. We do not insist that arguments on the grounds of national security should justify any and all R&D, all of the time. We simply urge full consideration of the issues.

With this background, let us turn to the specific problem of setting policy for the level and scope of defense R&D. Within the government, R&D programs have generally been organized around the missions of each of the major executive departments. This has led to a pluralistic pattern of support for the fields of science and technology. From an agency's viewpoint, this means that it supports any part of any field pertinent to its mission. From the scientists' viewpoint, it means that physicists, chemists, and biologists have often been supported simultaneously by several departments in terms of the apparent relevance of parts of their work to various missions. For instance, a physicist might be supported simultaneously by the National Science Foundation and the Department of Defense, and a biologist might be supported by the National Institute of Health and the Atomic Energy Commission. We endorse this strategy because it has tended to recognize the interrelationships of the underlying areas of knowledge, and has permitted each executive department to call upon a wide range of skills for its mission.

If each mission-agency were forced to narrow its R&D programs so that they fitted only the short-range definitions of a mission—as the Defense Department has been urged to do—the nation would soon have too little of the genuinely high-risk/high-gain R&D. We believe that defense R&D—like all of the other major mission-programs—should span a wide range, including selective investments in new high-potential technologies that do not necessarily meet a current, formally stated military requirement.

Reviewing a few examples of this approach may be helpful. Antisubmarine warfare (ASW) is likely to be a high priority area in our national security for many years. No matter what new concepts emerge in strategic deterrence, the submarine-based nuclear missile force will probably be the critical component because it is the least vulnerable to attack. But only if we explore all promising areas of ASW can we be sure that our force is, in fact, a secure and stable deterrent. R&D related to ASW includes many fields of underwater physics and oceanographic engineering, acoustics, design of underwater vehicles, special data and communications systems, marine biology and chemistry, together with the obvious requirements for advanced naval architecture and missile design. Progress in these investigations will continue to benefit civilian goals, national and international, related to resources offshore, in deep waters of the seas, and on the ocean bottom. Yet just as it is not now possible to forecast what the burgeoning "ocean gold rush" will produce for supplies of energy and food for coming generations, it is not now possible to state the formal military requirements for specific ASW equipment to be used in the future. We do know that this is a highly sensitive field strategically, and thus we would be wise to plan a broad defense R&D effort.

Comparable arguments can be drawn—in great detail—for work in a large number of fields including communications, electronics, some areas of the life sciences, propulsion, and computers. In each, there is both a distinctive reason for defense R&D—often overlapping but almost never duplicating the specific needs of other departments—and, at the same time, a reasonable prospect for obtaining results benefiting other national goals.

The effort in the technology base of defense research and development—about 20 percent of the total defense R&D budget, which in turn is ten percent of the overall Defense Department budget—should be managed in such a way as to provide the widest possible range of options, and to ensure that reliable choices can be made about what our national security truly requires in the way of production and deployment. With increasing arms control, which inevitably foreclose some options, there is an overriding need to find clearer answers to the questions, How much is enough now and what is truly required in the future? R&D can strengthen arms control by reducing the probability of technological surprise, building confidence in our assessments of the capabilities of potential enemies, and improving the efficiency of limited forces. Meeting all of these goals will demand a broad R&D program involving some of the most talented scientists and engineers in the country. In the final analysis, the success of defense R&D will be measured less by the number of new machines proved ready for production, than by the new knowledge proved adequate to validate our deterrent.

We close this section with a somewhat more subtle point. In the past, when the United States held overwhelming strategic and technical superiority, the principal psychological problem on our path toward effective deterrence was to establish credibility about our willingness to use force; without credibility, the power would have been politically useless. The resolution of the Cuban missile crisis seemed to demonstrate Russian perception of our credible power. Today, under conditions of strategic parity and technological stand-off, one clear way for us to reduce the risks of dangerous bluffing may be a renewed demonstration of vigorous technical leadership, because it will introduce an additional measure of caution in the Soviet Union's pursuit of political objectives around the world by military means.

Emphasis on Prototypes

So far, we have concentrated on the need to reassess strategic goals and to redefine tactical requirements in the light of the evolving international situation and the changing implications for R&D. We have also emphasized the vital importance of a broad defense effort in basic and applied research. For these three tasks, the key prerequisites are talented people with a willingness to work on the problems of national security and arms control.

But it is not enough simply to have clear goals for directing R&D, and to establish through research the underlying knowledge required to achieve these goals. Once a military need is clear and the general feasibility of meeting that need proved, then there must be a technically shrewd and fiscally prudent endeavor to bring a new system into the inventory. This process—the D in R&D—poses large-scale management problems which the United States has solved as well as any country. But we have made mistakes, too, and we have had to change our philosophy about such efforts as the costs of high-technology systems have risen dramatically. Out of the many controversial issues in the area of development management, we have selected two for discussion here and in the next section. The first concerns prototyping, which simply means building a complete model of a new system—such as a radar or even an aircraft—for thorough evaluation before making a commitment to purchase large quantities of the system.

As is well known, a substantial part of the current overall military budget is assigned to the vastly increased costs for military and civilian pay and to the routine operation of existing bases and equipment. Of the remainder—the more controllable part of the budget—most is devoted to the procurement, maintenance, and operation of relatively new, technically sophisticated military systems. The procurement of new systems has proved to be unpredictably expensive, as has been demonstrated by the F-111 fighter and the C-5A transport aircraft, which are now widely associated in the public mind with costly overruns. Such overruns were accepted as a more or less normal part of military business in the 1940s and 1950s. Since, however, the amount of money needed now is much larger, and the alternatives are more hotly debated, it is axiomatic that any future errors in cost estimates should and will be questioned sharply.

Much has been written about the origins of the overrun pattern. Part of it is caused by haste in going into tightly scheduled production of half-developed systems; part is the result of the unexpected escalation of costs of materials and labor; part is a symptom of the laxness that crept into such operations when systems costs were appreciably lower and fewer questions were asked; and, unfortunately, some overruns are caused by fuzziness in the original requirements, by not knowing clearly what is really needed.

Nevertheless, we must continue to probe new military systems in a highly imaginative way, both to attain capabilities which might be needed in emergencies and to acquire understanding of the technical opportunities which might be exploited by others. For example, it would be sheer madness for us to ignore the new laser systems having potential for vital communications as well as for offensive and defensive weapons that could make a critical difference in possible battle situations—even if we do not anticipate producing such systems for our own use in the near future. We must also construct and operate increasingly sophisticated surveillance satellites—which are, of course, essential to ensure the reliabilty of arms control agreements—in order to achieve a true assessment of their performance.

To resolve the dilemma created by the need to gain tighter control of production costs while continuing essential innovations, we should devote far more attention to the development of alternative prototype systems before deciding on what will undoubtedly be, in the future, a smaller number of commitments to extensive production. We should limit the initial procurement to a smaller number of models or, in some cases, of components which can be tested in a variety of ways before decisions are made on final utilization. Each model obviously would be expensive compared with a mass-produced version. Nevertheless, the process of creating prototypes would stimulate competitive innovations at many levels and places. It would lead to working devices which, after extensive tests, would form the basis for more coherent and less risky decisions about production. Prototyping also would help to avoid those cost overruns in procurement which occur when tightly scheduled plans for mass production are started without adequate information concerning the trade-offs in cost and performance of the actual system being produced.

Another important benefit of careful prototyping is the discipline it forces on planners to assess the degree to which increased efficiency will actually result from a new system. R&D must provide greater efficiency for our more limited military manpower, as we have commented earlier. Prototyping new equipment leads to more specific analyses of the costs and savings in manpower that might result from broad use of the candidate equipment.

The Defense Department's R&D management is already accelerating efforts in this direction. In fact, prototypes are now being developed for major new systems such as lightweight, less costly, high-performance fighter aircraft; new transport planes capable of short take-offs and landings on primitive fields, as a replacement for the older C-130 fleet; new heavy-lift helicopters using advanced technology and designed with the lessons learned in Vietnam about the enormous importance of helicopters in tactical situations; and a number of smaller electronic subsystems, for which the increasingly high production costs and low reliability of models already in the field have made it imperative to develop new equipment designed to a low price as well as to the essential, but minimum, military requirements. Despite this encouraging trend, we believe that there is more room for competitive prototyping and a great need for public support of this approach.

Assuming that the public would accept the higher R&D costs involved in full prototype development—which may, indeed, be doubtful in these unsettled times—perhaps the largest stumbling block to such a plan lies in acceptance of the principle by military leaders, who not without cause emphasize mainly the number of forces and systems in the field. Prototypes may point the way to achieving greater long-term effectiveness at lower overall cost. But a shift to more budgetary emphasis on prototypes and less on massive procurement might lead for a time to lower levels of new weapons in the field, a situation commanders do not welcome.

Associated with this drawback is the fact that prototype development will reduce, in the short run, large-scale employment by traditional industrial production organizations. As a result, emphasis on prototypes may represent an unattractive policy to Congressmen from districts which have benefited economically from massive procurement in the past.

Finally, we must amplify a problem we mentioned earlier. Prototyping cannot by itself answer the question of whether the Department of Defense has asked for the right system to meet a genuine need. Individual prototyping will determine whether a requested system is built and whether it works as planned. Competitive prototyping can also sharpen the understanding of major and minor trade-offs among contending designs. But prototyping clearly cannot resolve the larger problem of whether the right goals were set in the first place.

Nevertheless, the circumstances which will probably prevail in the future require the Pentagon to assure carefully managed R&D aimed at widely agreed upon goals in order to regain public confidence. Greater use of the prototyping approach appears to be a necessary step in this direction.

Independent Testing and Evaluation

Let us assume that a prototype has been developed and tested, that it passes muster technically, and that it fulfills a clear defense need. Suppose, for example, that the item is a new rifle, much lighter in weight and more accurate than existing models, perhaps fabricated of new materials so that it will also be more economical to operate and maintain; and suppose that the rifle is to be placed in production. At this stage—the final stage in R&D before passing into the presumably straightforward process of production—there must be a comprehensive final evaluation of the product to confirm that the production model has the required characteristics tested in the prototype. If this evaluation is not thorough, deficiencies in the rifle—perhaps in its maintainability—might not be discovered until thousands of rifles were in the hands of soldiers in the field.

At the present time, each military service procuring such a new system tends to play the role of both advocate and judge. It has spent years justifying the system, and must now try to be objective about whether the system in fact functions properly. The development and manufacturing contractors provide some critical judgment during testing and evaluation. But contractors are so tightly bound by detailed specifications and schedules, and so interested in the follow-on production profits, that their freedom and motive for action are severely limited. There is, in short, an obvious conflict of interest in judging one's own product.

The top management in the Department of Defense obviously provides a degree of independent in-house technical judgment on the performance of new systems. For example, the Office of the Director of Defense Research and Engineering maintains an overview of major R&D programs, and exercises considerable leverage when it feels that performance is questionable. Recently, this function has been strengthened through a series of special management reviews and through the appointment of a new Deputy Director of Defense Research and Engineering, who reports directly to the Secretary and Deputy Secretary on all major issues concerning the testing of new systems. But the government's main control has been budgetary rather than fully independent testing and evaluation. More important, the R&D groups within the military naturally tend to advocate the effectiveness of the results of their R&D.

In principle, optimal testing and evaluation require a sharper separation—of the incentives and the organization—between the judge and the advocate, between the tester and the developer/manufacturer. For example, it might be highly productive if, for a major contract in the latter stages of development leading to procurement, a parallel arrangement were made with a separate contractor to provide testing and evaluation services. In effect, the second contractor then becomes an independent judge of the performance of the first. The responsibility for administering these contracts for testing and evaluation could be assigned to an independent office attached to the Secretary of Defense and required to testify to Congress on its program. The office would serve in somewhat the manner in which the Office of Management and Budget serves the Executive Office in surveillance of the Federal budget. That is, it would be a quasi-independent voice in the evaluation of the performance of key projects.

Although the Defense Department has taken some actions across a fairly wide front to improve testing and evaluation, we think that even more emphasis is warranted. For instance, the use of "joint two-sided testing"—evaluating a new system against the "opposing" system of another service, such as the Air Force's anticarrier weapons against the Navy's carrier defenses—should be further increased and supplemented by panels of external consulting referees who would critically evaluate the design of tests and the reports of results. Furthermore, wherever feasible there should be realistic operational tests before high-rate production begins. In some current cases, this may require a decision to delay the scaling-up of production. But we think that virtually all of the arguable urgency about most programs is less important than the need to avoid unsatisfactory performance in the field.

In practice, a completely separate testing agency would not be feasible because some testing requires a very large commitment of men and ships or aircraft in order to carry out a realistic trial. The Navy certainly is not going to turn over a major fraction of the Sixth Fleet to a testing group for a long time, and the Congress certainly is not going to appropriate funds to set up a new, large operational force to be employed solely for testing. Nonetheless, the critical point is to assure independent management of the design, data collection, and data interpretation of testing.

Lest it be thought that this subject is merely a detail in management, it should be recalled that about $5 billion will be spent in fiscal year 1974 on about 500 major development projects. For each project, the quality of pre-production development, together with the thoroughness of operational testing, determine the effectiveness and suitability of the ultimate products purchased in large quantity and at enormous cost.

We will not dwell further on this matter, save to make two observations. First, we believe that more emphasis on hard-nosed, independent tests would help to rebuild Congressional and public confidence in defense procurement—by saving money and by assuring effective products. Second, this concept is already appreciated by the Department of Defense, but not by the R&D community in general. Thus, it is another challenge that we hope will be taken up by competent, nongovernmental technical groups who wish to help improve and control our national security effort.

5

Summary and Conclusions

We can summarize our themes by sketching a major three-part problem that has faced the officials responsible for defense R&D during the past several years. To begin with, the generation of scientists and engineers who worked on national security from 1940 to 1970 has been accustomed to a situation in which the United States possessed superiority in R&D funds, manpower, and facilities, as well as in the technical quality and number of advanced systems in the field. Today, however, our technological leadership is eroding fast as the results of the extraordinary Soviet investment in R&D over the last decade emerge. Many of our defense R&D administrators are not used to having to select among the best priorities under conditions in which resources are limited. In the past, we could and did invest in virtually every promising area, and we knew that the competition was not pressing. Now, we cannot afford to cover all the bets, and we know the competition is strong and productive. This is our first problem.

A second, related problem arises from the fact that the Congress tends to be skeptical about longer range R&D—which, in the official

44

jargon, lies within the Research and Exploratory Development budgets. Indeed, laws have been passed to limit defense funding to those R&D projects that can be shown to be specifically relevant to defined, current operational needs. Such rules are thoroughly reasonable in principle; but when interpreted too narrowly, they may result in too little exploratory work being supported. When this trend is combined with the unfortunate tendency of the Department of Defense to classify far too much R&D, the one crucial capability that the US still possesses—a magnificent national research base, which is strengthened and disciplined by continuous, open criticism in professional circles—cannot be fully utilized. We should add that this problem is shared by other departments, such as Commerce and Health, Education and Welfare, whose basic or long-range R&D is also limited by Congress.

The third problem stems from the circumstance that both the Defense Department and the Congress tend to underestimate the funding needed to remove risks from the major engineering development of new systems. Full-scale prototyping and thorough testing and evaluation, along the lines we have emphasized, are costly. They usually are highly cost-effective over a long period because they eliminate most of the sources of cost overruns, schedule slippages, and the underfulfillment of performance goals. Nevertheless, with funding tight, the Defense Department and the Congress too often fail to support these needs. This is almost always a false economy.

These three problems in the management of defense R&D—dramatic changes in the nature of the choices we face in a competitive environment, legislative skepticism about the relevance of long-range R&D, and keen pressure to restrain the larger budgets required for the prototyping and testing necessary to sharpen short-range R&D— cry out for the attention of our most able scientists, engineers, and technical managers.

Conclusions

We have tried to touch on some of the sensitive issues that must be confronted in a frank, rational debate on the role of R&D in building international security. The national divisions caused by the war in Vietnam, a lingering preoccupation with obsolescent theories of strategic deterrence, the present national inclination toward retrenchment coupled to some blindness about the possible risks in this course, the hopes for rapid progress toward reliable arms control —all these factors must be taken into account in formulating our defense R&D program.

Yet, at a moment when so much must be done by way of assessing our own options and when Soviet willingness to negotiate in SALT seems inconsistent with the continued Soviet build-up of its military R&D base and its worldwide conventional forces, much of the intellectual community in our country has chosen to shun the problems of national security. This short essay will, perhaps, provoke interest in the issues and broader participation in more complete assessments.

We believe that long-range defense R&D represents a crucial investment toward preserving a margin of safety in deterrence, assuring reliable arms controls, and maintaining a credible capability for flexible responses to tactical conflicts that the US cannot ignore. The balance of defense R&D effort should be tilted in the direction of broader exploratory efforts and fewer large-scale developments, although we recognize the importance of certain current major programs such as the strategic submarine force. Further, we think that defense R&D does not drain an exorbitant amount of technical talent from work on other national goals; in fact, when managed astutely and carried out openly, its pay-offs often ripple out to benefit many other national programs.

In the future, national attention to defense R&D should be revivified by stronger contact with the first-rank scientific and engineering community, by a sharp reduction in the scope of secrecy, and by closer central management. As an agenda for discussion and action, we propose that five specific areas receive the highest priority: (1) the analysis of strategic options—to chart flexible paths for US policy, especially in arms control and strategic deterrence; (2) the reassessment of tactical needs—to increase the effectiveness of our smaller and more highly paid general forces, and to understand the implications of the Nixon Doctrine; (3) the maintenance of a broad research and technology base—to ensure that critical technologies for all of our national interests are explored; (4) the concentration on prototyping—to stimulate competitive innovation, control costs, measure risk and performance, and rebuild confidence in decisions to go into procurement; and (5) the establishment of a system of more independent testing and evaluation—to tighten the process of transition from development to procurement, and to improve the quality of the products bought for our forces.

Appendix

During the past fifteen years, a number of analysts and journalists have assessed the role of the Defense Department's spending on various components of the national and international economy. Despite many lengthy publications and debates, there have been few authoritative compilations of the general facts and trends, and even fewer reviews of the R&D situation as a special case within the complicated pattern of national activities. Hence, it might be helpful to examine the following data and arguments published by the Department of Defense in July 1972.

This appendix is a slightly abbreviated and edited version of the chapter on "The Impact (of defense spending) Upon Technology and Industry," in *The Economics of Defense Spending: A Look at Realities* (Washington: Department of Defense, July 1972). It was prepared by the Comptroller of the Department of Defense, and is available upon request from that office.

We do not subscribe to every argument offered in this excerpt, nor have we independently analyzed all of the economic data shown. But we believe that this presentation, on balance, provides an extremely important survey of the role of defense R&D in the American economy.

As a single example, there is a popular myth that defense places an inordinate drain on the nation's research and development resources; but the fact is that defense-related R&D is smaller in real terms now than in 1958 or any year since.

We believe that such facts must be confronted squarely in any discussion of national defense policy and the role of defense R&D in future planning for international security.

Research and development

The total US R&D effort for selected years is summarized in table 7-1. These figures are from the National Science Foundation. For those familiar with Department of Defense program and budget summaries, it should be emphasized that table 7-1 shows calendar years (not fiscal years) and that the "defense-related" figures include R&D costs financed by the Atomic Energy Commission as well as DoD costs.

Note that the total US R&D effort grows from $5.2 billion in 1953 to an estimated $28 billion in 1972. Defense R&D more than doubled from 1953 to 1958. However, from 1958 to 1972 total US R&D grows from $10.9 billion to $28 billion, including:

• Defense-related R&D growth	2.4 billion (42%)
• Space-related R&D growth	2.8 billion (2,800%)
• All other R&D growth	11.9 billion (233%)
For a total US R&D growth of	17.1 billion (157%)

These figures make it very difficult to conclude that other R&D efforts have been starved for funds to make room for defense efforts. The same point is demonstrated if we look at percentage shares:

Percent of total US R&D effort

	1953	1958	1963	1968	1972
Defense-related	47.5%	52.0%	40.6%	33.9%	29.0%
Space-related	.8	1.0	13.7	13.2	10.4
Subtotal	48.3	53.0	54.3	47.1	39.4
All other	51.7	47.0	45.7	52.9	60.6
Total	100.0	100.0	100.0	100.0	100.0

Source: National Science Foundation, *National Patterns of R&D Resources, 1953-1972,* NSF 72-300, December 1971, p. 34.

In 1958, defense R&D was greater than all other US R&D combined. Today, other R&D efforts exceed defense by a factor of 2½ to 1. Setting aside the space program, defense R&D was nearly equal to all other US R&D as late as 1963; in 1972, all other R&D—excluding space—exceeds defense by a factor of better than 2 to 1.

Table 7-1

Source of US R&D Funds by Sector
($ Billions)

	1953	1958	1963	1968	1972 (Est.)
Federal Government:					
Defense-related	$ 2.5	$ 5.7	$ 7.1	$ 8.5	$ 8.1
Space-related	−	.1	2.4	3.3	2.9
All other	.2	1.0	1.8	3.1	4.2
Total, Federal Government	$ 2.8	$ 6.8	$11.2	$15.0	$15.2
Non-Federal:					
Industry	$ 2.2	$ 3.7	$ 5.4	$ 9.0	$11.3
Universities and colleges	.2	.3	.5	.8	1.1
Other nonprofit institutions	.1	.1	.2	.3	.4
Total, Non-Federal	$ 2.4	$ 4.1	$ 6.2	$10.2	$12.8
Total, US R&D	$ 5.2	$10.9	$17.4	$25.2	$28.0
Summaries:					
Defense-related	$ 2.5	$ 5.7	$ 7.1	$ 8.5	$ 8.1
All other	2.7	5.2	10.3	16.6	19.9
Total, US R&D	$ 5.2	$10.9	$17.4	$25.2	$28.0
Defense-related and space	$ 2.5	$ 5.8	$ 9.4	$11.8	$11.0
All other	2.7	5.1	7.9	13.3	17.0
Total, US R&D	$ 5.2	$10.9	$17.4	$25.2	$28.0

The column group is headed "Calendar Years".

Source: National Patterns of R&D Resources, 1953-1972, pp. 32 and 34.

Table 7-2

Summary of US R&D Funds by Sector
(In billions of CY 1958 dollars)

	1953	1958	1963	1968	1972 (Est.)
		Calendar Years			
Federal Government:					
Defense-related	$ 2.8	$ 5.7	$ 6.6	$ 7.0	$ 5.5
Space-related	–	.1	2.2	2.7	2.0
All other	.3	1.0	1.7	2.6	2.8
Total, Federal Government	3.1	6.8	10.5	12.3	10.4
Non-Federal:					
Industry	2.5	3.7	5.1	7.4	7.7
Universities and colleges	.2	.3	.5	.7	.7
Other nonprofit institutions	.1	.1	.2	.3	.3
Total, Non-Federal	2.8	4.1	5.7	8.3	8.7
Total, US R&D	5.9	10.9	16.2	20.6	19.1
Summaries:					
Defense-related	2.8	5.7	6.6	7.0	5.5
All other	3.1	5.2	9.6	13.6	13.5
Total, US R&D	5.9	10.9	16.2	20.6	19.1
Defense-related and space	2.8	5.8	8.8	9.7	7.5
All other	3.1	5.1	7.4	10.9	11.6
Total, US R&D	5.9	10.9	16.2	20.6	19.1

Source: Foregoing table, deflated with GNP deflator. NSF also uses GNP deflator for stating totals in constant prices (*National Patterns of R&D Resources, 1953-1972*, p. 2), but uses a CY 1967 base. CY 1958 base is used here for consistency with other data. Use of a different base year does not alter relationships among the years. Rounded figures may not add to rounded totals.

R&D trends in constant prices. There is a great deal more significance in the figures in table 7-2, which are in constant (CY 1958) prices. Note that defense R&D, in constant prices, was $5.7 billion in 1958 and is $5.5 billion of 1972—below the 1958 level. All of the real growth in US R&D capacity since 1958, and a bit more, is thus available for civilian pursuits. It is also significant to note that the total US R&D effort drops from $20.6 billion in 1968 to $19.1 billion in 1972.

Here are the increases in US R&D in recent periods, drawn from table 7-2:

Increases in US R&D Spending
($ in billions at CY 1958 prices)

	Defense	Defense & space combined	All other R&D	Total US R&D
1953-58	$+2.9 (104%)	$+3.0 (107%)	$+2.0 (65%)	$+5.0 (85%)
1958-63	$+ .9 (16%)	$+3.0 (52%)	$+2.3 (45%)	$+5.3 (49%)
1963-68	$+ .4 (6%)	$+ .9 (10%)	$+3.5 (47%)	$+4.4 (27%)
1968-72	$—1.5 (—21%)	$—2.2 (—23%)	$+ .7 (6%)	$—1.5 (—7%)

These figures effectively refute the contentions of some analysts that defense has preempted our R&D resources, leaving practically nothing for civilian or domestic efforts. Consider this contention in light of the facts:

- The most rapid growth in domestic/industrial R&D (this excludes the space program) was 65%, from 1953 to 1958—the period of the greatest defense buildup.

- Second place for growth in domestic/industrial R&D goes to the 47% in the 1963-68 period—the war buildup period.

- On the other hand, domestic/industrial R&D grew hardly at all from 1968 to 1972, while the defense and space programs were being sharply curtailed.

If defense (and perhaps the space program) was hoarding all the talent and resources, leaving practically none for domestic and industrial applications—then these other areas should have been stagnant from 1953 to 1963; in fact, they grew at a very healthy rate—faster than defense, as a matter of fact. By the same token, the first hypothesis would require domestic/industrial R&D to skyrocket after 1968, when defense and space cut back; to put it mildly, this didn't happen.

Table 7-3

*Source of Funds for R&D Performed in Colleges and
Universities and at Associated Federally-Funded
Research and Development Centers (FFRDC's)*
($ Millions)

	1953	1956	1961	1964	1968	1972
R&D Performed in Colleges and Universities						
Federal Government:						
Defense	$NA	$122	$ 198	$ 295	$ 307	$ 246
Space	NA	1	15	90	138	105
All other programs	NA	90	287	531	1,127	1,399
Total, Federal Government	138	213	500	916	1,572	1,750
Industry	19	29	40	41	55	65
Universities, colleges, and state and local government	151	204	371	555	841	1,060
Other nonprofit institutions	26	34	58	83	131	175
Total R&D performed in colleges and universities	334	480	969	1,595	2,599	3,050
R&D Performed in Associated FFRDC's						
Defense	NA	168	330	340	363	367
Space	NA	–	26	87	104	153
All other programs	NA	26	54	202	252	255
Total R&D in FFRDC's	121	194	410	629	719	775
Total R&D Performed in Colleges, Universities and Associated FFRDC's						
Defense	NA	290	528	635	670	613
Space	NA	1	41	177	242	258
All other Federal programs	NA	116	341	733	1,379	1,654
Total Federal funding	259	407	910	1,545	2,291	2,525
All other funding	196	267	469	679	1,027	1,300

Total R&D, Colleges, Universities and Associated FFRDC's	455	674	1,379	2,224	3,318	3,825

Defense as percent of:

Federal funding, excluding FFRDC's	57.3%	39.6%	32.2%	19.5%	14.1%
Federal funding, including FFRDC's	71.3%	58.0%	41.1%	29.2%	24.3%
Total R&D at colleges and universities	25.4%	20.4%	18.5%	11.8%	8.1%
Total R&D at colleges, universities and FFRDC's	43.0%	38.3%	28.6%	20.2%	16.0%

Source: National Patterns of R&D Resources, 1953-1972, pp. 24-25, except for breakdowns of Federal Government funds. These were distributed on the basis of agency percentages furnished by NSF staff. The defense figures include all costs financed by DoD, plus 80% of all costs financed by AEC through 1964 and 50% thereafter.

Funding of research performed in colleges and universities is summarized in table 7-3. This is an especially important indication of the trend that R&D is taking. The table shows the source of funds for work performed at colleges and universities *per se* and, separately, the Federally Funded Research and Development Centers (FFRDC's) which are administered by individual schools or university consortia.

It is important to note the sharp falloff in the defense (including AEC) proportions of the university R&D totals shown at the bottom of table 7-3. Considering the overall R&D effort at colleges and universities:

- Defense falls from 43% of the total in 1956 to 16% in 1972, if the FFRDC's are included.

- Setting aside the FFRDC's, the defense share drops from 25.4% in 1956 to 8.1% in 1972.

As to that part of the R&D at colleges and universities that is financed by the Federal Government:

- Defense falls from 71.3% of the total in 1956 to 24.3% in 1972 if the FFRDC's are included.

- Setting aside the FFRDC's, the defense share drops from 57.3% in 1956 to 14.1% in 1972. In FY 1973, this figure will fall to 10.7%.[1]

---

[1] *FY 1973* Budget, Special Analyses, p. 283. The figures on an obligation basis were used, and it was estimated that 50% of AEC R&D involves military applications.

Table 7-4 presents the data in terms of constant prices. The trend here is similar in many respects to the overall US R&D trend. Note that the defense level in 1972 is below the 1961 level and above the 1956 level. In 1956, defense programs accounted for $309 million of university R&D work; all other programs for $408 million. In 1972, defense-related effort is $420 million, compared to $2.2 billion for all other R&D. Over this period, defense work is up 36%, all other work by 439%.

It is also significant to note that university R&D effort drops, in real terms, from 1968 to 1972, following the overall trend.

Once again, it is difficult to discern any pattern of defense dominance that is so obvious to a few critics.

Table 7-4

Sources of Funds for R&D Performed in Colleges and Universities and at Associated Federally-Funded Research and Development Centers (FFRDC's)
(In millions of CY 1958 dollars)

	1953	1956	1961	1964	1968	1972
R&D Performed in Colleges and Universities						
Federal Government:						
Defense	$NA	$130	$ 189	$ 271	$ 251	$ 168
Space	NA	1	14	83	113	72
All other	NA	96	274	488	921	958
Total, Federal Government	156	227	478	842	1,285	1,199
Non-Federal sources	222	284	448	624	840	890
Total R&D performed in colleges and universities	378	511	926	1,466	2,125	2,089
R&D Performed in Associated FFRDC's						
Defense	NA	179	315	312	297	251
Space	NA	–	25	80	85	105
All other	NA	28	52	186	206	175
Total R&D in FFRDC's	137	207	392	578	588	531

*Total R&D Performed
in Colleges, Universi-
ties and Associated
FFRDC's*

Defense	NA	309	505	584	548	420
Space	NA	1	39	163	198	177
All other Federal programs	NA	123	326	674	1,127	1,133
Total Federal funding	293	433	870	1,420	1,873	1,730
Non-Federal sources	222	284	448	624	840	890
Total R&D in colleges, universities and associated FFRDC's	515	717	1,318	2,044	2,713	2,620

Source: Table 7-3, converted to constant prices using GNP deflator.

Manpower. Additional perspective is added by the figures on earned degrees in science and engineering, which follow:

Earned degrees in science and engineering
(bachelor, master, and doctor) in thousands

1953/54	100.0	1958/59	141.1	1963/64	192.7	1968/69	308.7
1954/55	100.0	1959/60	147.0	1964/65	209.0	1969/70	331.0
1955/56	107.0	1960/61	151.0	1965/66	222.0		
1956/57	119.0	1961/62	159.0	1966/67	243.0		
1957/58	130.9	1962/63	171.5	1967/68	271.7		

1954-58 Avg. 111.4 1959-63 Avg. 153.9 1964-68 Avg. 227.7 1969-70 Avg. 319.9

Source: HEW, Office of Education.

Defense R&D, it will be recalled, grew sharply (in constant prices) from 1953 to 1958, and domestic/industrial R&D also enjoyed its greatest growth during this period. This was fueled by (a) an average of 111,400 science and engineering graduates per year, as shown above, and (b) a sharp increase in the proportion of natural scientists and engineers engaged in R&D[2]. Since then, defense has become a net exporter of R&D, and the number of graduates has approximately tripled. One can scarcely conclude from this that defense is hoarding our R&D capacity.

Since about 1964, R&D employment has not been growing as fast as available manpower; the proportion of all natural scientists and engineers engaged in R&D has been declining.[3] Moreover, since 1969, there has been an absolute decline in professional employment, as follows:

---

[2] *National Patterns of R&D Resources, 1953-1972*, p. 9.
[3] *Ibid.*

Full-Time Equivalent Scientists and Engineers Employed in R&D
(in thousands)

| | Total | Approximate Breakdown | |
		Defense-Related	All Other
1954	236.8	114.1	122.7
1958	354.7	184.4	170.3
1961	425.2	209.2	216.0
1965	496.5	160.4	336.1
1968	550.6	186.6	364.0
1969	559.4	188.0	371.4
1970	544.6	159.0	385.6
1971	519.4	149.1	370.3

Source: Totals from *National Patterns of R&D Resources, 1953-1972*, p. 34. Breakdown is based upon spending percentages also shown on page 34.

Scientific and engineering employment in R&D grew by 188,400 (80%) from 1954 to 1961; from 1961 to 1968, employment grew by just 125,400 (29%) and has fallen since then. Meanwhile, as we have seen, the number of graduates has tripled. Once again, there is no evidence that defense is hoarding or preempting our R&D capabilities.

As indicated in table 7-2, domestic/industrial R&D has grown by $6.5 billion at constant prices (127%) from 1958 to 1972, while defense-related R&D was dropping slightly. The figures just presented indicate quite clearly that domestic/industrial R&D could have grown by a much greater amount if there was a real demand.

All of these figures point to the same conclusion, and in fact they allow for no other—there *is* no shortage of R&D capacity caused by allocating the lion's share of these resources to defense. In fact, there is no shortage at all. It is commonplace today to observe that there are 72 applicants for every job opening requiring a Ph.D., while no one can hire a plumber. There has been high-level government concern for a considerable period with the high unemployment rates among scientists and engineers. On September 15, 1970, for example, the Director of Office of Management and Budget wrote to several cabinet officers seeking cooperation in an effort to ". . . take advantage of the opportunity, presented by the reduction in defense needs, to redeploy our technological resources in the solution of domestic problems." (Memo, September 15, 1970, from OMB Director George P. Shultz to Secretaries Romney, Richardson, Hodgson, Laird, Volpe, Hardin, Hickel and Mitchell, NASA Administrator Paine, and AEC Chairman Seaborg, subject: "Employment of Scientists and Engineers During the Transition to Lower Defense Budget.")

Growth in domestic/industrial R&D. If there is no R&D supply problem, then, why hasn't domestic/industrial R&D grown more rapidly—especially in recent years? We don't know, and we haven't met anyone who does. We can offer a few suggestions however.

First of all, it doesn't appear to be a money problem. With respect to the Federal R&D effort (excluding space and defense), table 7-2 shows a very sharp pattern of real growth through 1968, then a virtual halt. Meanwhile, total spending is rising very rapidly. Here are the figures on increases in Federal social and economic spending (all Federal spending less defense, debt interest, VA, NASA and international affairs) related to increases in R&D spending in those areas:

	($ in billions)		
	Increase in Federal, social & economic spending	*Increase in R&D spending, same agencies*	*% of increase allocated to R&D*
1953-58	$ 9.8	$ .8	8.2%
1958-63	15.6	.8	5.1%
1963-68	32.6	1.3	4.0%
1968-72	55.2	1.1	2.0%

Source: Tables 7-1 and OMB historical tables.

Had these other agencies allocated 8.2% of the 1968-72 increase to R&D, as they did in 1953-58, their R&D level would be nearly equal to defense R&D today.

For the economy as a whole, a much smaller share of the real GNP increment has been allocated to R&D, as shown in the following table:[4]

	(In CY 1958, $ billions)		
	Increase in GNP, excluding Defense and NASA	*Increase in domestic/ industrial R&D*	*% of increase allocated to R&D*
1953-58	$ 50.3	$ 2.0	4.0%
1958-63	89.8	2.3	2.6%
1963-68	134.1	3.5	2.6%
1968-72	84.8	.7	.8%

Once again, a progressively smaller share of the GNP increment is being allocated to R&D.

The National Science Foundation has attributed these trends to "the recent economic slowdown."[5] This may be, but we would have to observe

---

[4] Increase in GNP from Department of Commerce data. Increase in R&D spending from Table 7-2.
[5] *National Patterns of R&D Resources, 1953-1972,* p. 2.

that there was a much deeper slump in the 1953-58 period. Unemployment was 2.9% in 1953, 5.5% in 1954, 4.1% to 4.4% in 1955-57, and rose to 6.8% in 1958—compared to 3.6% in 1968, 3.5% in 1969, 4.9% in 1970, and 5.9% to 6% in 1971-72. Real GNP, setting aside space and defense, grew at 2.7% annually, 1953-58, compared to 3.2% annually from 1968 to 1972.[6]

Corporate profits after taxes rose from $20.4 billion in 1953 to $22.2 billion in 1958—a rise of $1.8 billion, or 8.8%. From 1968 to the first quarter of 1972 (at annual rates), the rise was from $47.8 billion to $52.5 billion—$4.7 billion, or 9.8%. This offers no explanation of why domestic/industrial R&D in real terms grew 65% from 1953 to 1958, and only 6% from 1968 to 1972.

It is a striking fact that defense/space and domestic/industrial R&D tend to be complementary, rather than competitive. Some analysts' thesis, of course, is that we must choose one or the other. For reasons that we don't understand, we seem to get both or neither. Thus, domestic/industrial R&D grew most rapidly when defense and space were growing, then levelled off when defense and space fell. There may be inter-relationships, spin-offs, and feedbacks to a greater extent than is generally assumed.

There are many other possibiilties. Perhaps there are some economic interrelationships that are not at present understood. It may be that R&D follows a cycle of its own, related to the thrust of discoveries and innovations, and that we are in a relatively quiet period at present.

As we said at the beginning of this section, we don't know why domestic/industrial R&D has not grown faster, especially in recent years. Certainly there is no supply problem, and plausible economic or financial explanations do not come readily to mind. For reasons that are not clear, business and other government agencies seem to be allocating much less to R&D.

In summary, a few observers begin with two simple facts: (1) We have brownouts and other indications of a need for the application of more scientific and engineering skills to domestic and industrial problems, and (2) defense is a large user of scientific and engineering skills. From this, they conclude that we have these problems *because* defense is using scientific and engineering skills. This is, to put it mildly, illogical. They are confusing supply with demand and distribution. The fact is that there are plenty of R&D resources available, and an immense capacity for growth. It is simply not necessary to cut billions out of defense R&D funds in order to expand domestic/industrial R&D efforts.

---

[6] *Statistical Abstract*, 1971, Table 791, p. 501.

Energy and transportation

First, let's consider the matter of electrical energy. Here are the figures on total US electric power production and capacity:

	1940	1950	1960	1970
Production (billions of kw hours)	180	389	842	1,638
Capacity (million kw)	51	83	186	360

Source: Statistical Abstract, 1971, p. 497.

It's a little hard to conclude that defense and space programs, or anything else for that matter, have been impeding the expansion of electric power production. Why are there brownouts, then? Obviously, because the demand for electric power has been growing at a phenomenal rate. Residential uses have been leading the way, growing much more rapidly than commercial and industrial uses.

What has happened, in short, is that huge amounts have been invested in both turbines and toasters, and there has probably been an imbalance —too much for toasters, too little for turbines. What has that to do with the defense and space programs? The basic problem is that our demands for electric energy have grown at a phenomenal rate, because of the development and sale of a wide variety of appliances that use a great deal of electricity. This problem could not exist, of course, if the defense and space programs had in fact preempted our durable goods production. Meanwhile, the construction of electrical generation facilities has been inhibited, largely by environmental considerations.

Some observers make complimentary references to Germany and Japan, ". . . where the diversion of technical talent to military purposes has been restricted." They don't mention that the US consumption of all sources of energy per capita (coal equivalent) is about 3.8 times that of Japan and 2.2 times that of the Federal Republic of Germany. As to electrical energy, the ratios are 3.0 to 1 (US to Japan) and 2.3 to 1 (US to Federal Republic of Germany).[7] At those rates, we could avoid brownouts for a long time to come.

---

[7] *Ibid.*, p. 808.

As to transportation, where do we put our horses? Here's where:

Total Horsepower of all US Prime Movers
(in millions)

	1940	1950	1960	1970
Automotive (cars, trucks, buses, and motorcycles)	2,511	4,404	10,367	19,325
Nonautomotive:				
Factories	22	33	42	54
Mines	7	22	35	45
Railroads	92	111	47	54
Merchant ships and sailing vessels	9	23	24	22
Farms	70	165	240	301
Electric control stations	54	80	217	435
Aircraft	7	22	37	183
Total, nonautomotive	262	464	641	1,094
Grand total	2,773	4,868	11,008	20.419

Source: Statistical Abstract, 1971, p. 495.

In case we hadn't noticed before, these figures ought to convince us that Americans love automobiles. Even in 1940—before there was a military-industrial complex—automotive horsepower exceeded that of railroads by 27 to 1. By 1970, the ratio had grown to 358 to 1.

In 1971, Americans spent $37.6 billion on the purchase of new and used cars, and spent an average of $1,189 per year operating 89.9 million automobiles—over $100 billion per year.[8] Highway construction costs were $6.5 billion in 1970.[9] The operating revenues of truck lines were $13.5 billion in 1969, and of business $1 billion; domestic scheduled airlines, incidentally, had operating revenues of $6.4 billion in 1970.[10] In 1970, a total of 8.2 million new motor vehicles were sold, including 6.5 million cars at $14.5 billion (included within the $33.8 billion already mentioned), and 1.7 million trucks and buses at $4.5 billion. 1970 was a low year; the 1965-69 average was 10.2 million units per year.[11]

While all this was going on, the railroad area was quieter—to put it mildly. Total operating revenues of the railroads were $12 billion in 1969;[12] total expenditures for new railroad plant and equipment are

---

[8] *Ibid.*, pp. 534, 537.
[9] *Ibid.*, p. 526.
[10] *Ibid.*, p. 524.
[11] *Ibid.*, p. 534.
[12] *Ibid.*, p. 524.

steady at about $1.8 billion per year from 1969 to 1972.[13] The railroads acquired just 240 new passenger cars in 1969, compared to 65 in 1968, 251 in 1960, and 1,078 in 1950.[14]

The United States in 1969 had 103.9 million motor vehicles in use, compared to 15.1 million in Japan and 13.1 million in West Germany. On a per capita basis, for the total population, the US had 3.5 times as many cars as the Japanese and 2.4 times as many as the West Germans; for the economically active populations, the per capita ratios were 4.2 to 1 (US/Japan) and 2.6 to 1 (US/West Germany).[15]

The love of the American for his automobile, and his propensity to lavish huge amounts of money on it, is truly one of the phenomena of our time. It is easy to point out that it is illogical to spend so much on automobiles and so little on mass transit and other forms of transportation. This tendency has made many strong men weep—from city planners and urbanologists to ecologists, environmentalists and transportation specialists. There have been studies galore, pointing out, for example, that just the gasoline we burn up in traffic jams costs enough to provide a large part of the funds needed for mass transit. It has been pointed out that investing just a fraction of the well over $100 billion we devote to automobiles and trucks each year could be much better applied to other forms of transit. All to little avail.

The impact upon American industry

Defense impact by sector. In addition to hoarding our technical talent and plundering the infrastructure, some critics allege defense has corrupted American industry for three decades. Having grown accustomed to producing largely for defense needs, these critics explain, it is little wonder that American industries across the board have drifted into incompetence. For example, Melman has stated that "about 20,000 industrial firms participate in the military-industrial system"[16] and are being corrupted to varying degrees.

It is important, then, to have some appreciation of the size of defense relative to the American economy. In calendar 1972, GNP is estimated at $1,145.5 billion, and defense purchases are $75.8 billion, or 6.6% of the GNP. That figure in itself ought to suggest a little caution in attributing such a widespread and catastrophic impact to defense programs. This point becomes even sharper if we consider the breaking of the CY 1972 GNP by major type of product:

[13] *Economic Report of the President,* January 1972, p. 239.
[14] *Statistical Abstract,* 1971, p. 547.
[15] *Ibid.,* pp. 794, 795, 808, 819.
[16] Industrial College of the Armed Forces, *Perspectives in Defense Management,* Spring 1972, p. 8.

| | ($ in billions) | | | |
	Total goods and services produced	*Defense takes*	*Re-mainder*	*Defense as % of total*
Goods and services produced in private sector:				
Durable goods, except aircraft and ordnance	$ 195.3	$ 9.4	$ 185.9	4.8%
Nondurable goods	317.2	4.5	312.7	1.4%
Services	325.1	10.6	314.5	3.3%
Structures	127.8	1.5	126.3	1.2%
Subtotal	965.4	26.0	939.4	2.7%
Durable goods (aircraft & ordnance)	24.2	13.3	10.9	55.0%
Total goods and services produced in private sector	989.6	39.3	950.3	4.0%
Federal, state & local govt. payrolls	155.9	36.5	119.4	23.4%
Total GNP, CY 1972	1,145.5	75.8	1,069.7	6.6%

The image that is created by "defense purchases" of $75.8 billion is that of a mountain of manufactured products—$75.8 billion worth of elaborate, expensive hardware. As the figures demonstrate, this simply isn't so. Nearly half of that $75.8 billion represents pay of military and civil service personnel ($36.5 billion, as shown). The services of these people are included in the GNP, and the Department of Defense "purchases" this part of the GNP by paying salaries.

The GNP represents the value of all the goods *and services* produced each year. The main components, as the table shows, are goods (durable and nondurable); commercial services (transportation, utilities, car repairs, etc.); construction; and governmental services—essentially the pay of schoolteachers, firemen, soldiers, sailors, airmen, policemen, tax collectors, judges, and all people on the public payroll. These, collectively, comprise the total output (of goods and services) of the American economy.

The table just presented shows how much of the output of these various types of goods and services are being taken by defense this year. Beginning with the total, NIA defense purchases are $75.8 billion, or 6.6% of the GNP. Nearly half of this, however, involves pay. This is a large percentage (23.4%) of the total public payroll. As we have noted elsewhere, this represents the smallest defense share of the public payroll since before Pearl Harbor. This part of the defense budget has nothing to do with defense contracting with industry.

Considering the goods and services produced by the private sector of the economy, then, defense takes $39.3 billion—4%. As the table shows, there is a heavy concentration in two Standard Industrial Classification (SIC) codes: aircraft and ordnance (which includes missiles). Note that these two industries—where defense clearly dominates, taking over half of the total product—are a very small part of the economy. Setting these two industries aside for the moment, we find that defense purchases account for just 2.7% of the output of goods and services of the private sector. More specifically, here is what that means:

- Of the total output of durable goods, excluding aircraft and ordnance, of $195.3 billion, defense took $9.4 billion—4.8%. This covers items such as cars, trucks, industrial equipment, appliances and office machines; on the defense side, it would cover such items plus military vehicles, weapons, ships and electronics.

- As to nondurable goods, clothing, food, gasoline, household supplies, etc.—defense takes 1.4% of the total.

- Services include transportation, communications, other utilities, repairs, wholesaling and retailing, etc. The defense share is 3.3%.

- As to structures—construction—the defense share is 1.3%.

These amounts, and these percentages, apply to 98% of the private sector of the economy—all but aircraft and ordnance. What this means, then, is that for the vast bulk of the private sector of the economy, defense is just a customer. A large customer, to be sure, sometimes the biggest single customer—but hardly a dominant factor, unless 2.7% equals dominance.

In short, the depiction of the American economy as largely and increasingly dependent upon defense work, picking up bad habits and losing its zip in the process, is wildly incorrect. Look at the table again. We are discussing $965.4 billion in goods and services produced in the private sector of the economy. When we put $26 billion in defense purchases into that kind of an arena, we shouldn't be thinking about dominance. Defense amounts to 27 cents of every 10 dollars; for that kind of money, one might deserve to be listened to, but one shouldn't have any ideas about running the show.

It is sometimes necessary to remind people—military fundamentalists most of all—that the American economy is indeed immense. National wealth (tangible assets) was estimated at $3.1 trillion in 1968. This included $1.5 trillion in structures—at recent rates of military construction, it would take more than a thousand years to match that. Equipment on hand (producer and consumer durables) was valued at $611 billion, and inventories were valued at $216 billion more. This total of $827 billion in goods (in 1968) is equivalent to some 40 times the annual goods procured for defense—hard goods, consumables, and all. Factory sales of new motor vehicles were 11.1 million in 1965, and have been in the 8-10 million range each year since, with indications that the 11.1 million record may soon be exceeded. In 1970, 7.1 million home laundry units (washers and driers) were sold; 19.7 million "other major appliances," such as dishwashers, freezers, ranges, and refrigerators; 75.1 million units under the heading of electric housewares (coffeemakers, irons, mixers, toasters, etc.); and 20.7 million air treatment units—air conditioners and fans. There were 3.7 million miles of highway in the US in 1969, and in the Federal system alone some 11,000 miles of new highway were completed in that year.[17]

The total labor force at June 30, 1972, was 88.8 million. Public employment, military and civilian, Federal, state, and local took 15.8 million of these people, leaving 73 million for the private sector. Of these, 4.7 million were unemployed, leaving 68.3 million employed in the private sector. And of that 68.3 million, the production of goods and services for defense required 1.9 million—2.8% of the total.

Note the figures in table 7-5 for 1972. Total durable goods production is $219.5 billion, of which $196.8 billion goes for civilian and domestic pursuits. Similarly, nondefense construction is $126.2 billion. The defense program simply does not begin to match the . magnitudes we have been describing. Whatever superlative one chooses to apply to the defense budget, he must reserve another, several orders of magnitude greater, to apply to the economy. And whenever one is describing the relationship of defense to the economy, "dominance" is not the word to use.

---

[17] Figures in this paragraph are from the *Statistical Abstract*, 1971, pp. 328, 534, 718-719, and 527.

TABLE 7-5
Defense Purchases and GNP by Major Type of Product
($ in billions)

Calendar years	Aircraft & ord. (incl. missiles)	All other durable goods	Total durable goods	Non-durable goods	Federal, state & local payrolls	Other Services	Structures	Total GNP
1953 US total	$ 16.8	$ 62.6	$ 79.4	$124.8	$ 35.5	$ 83.3	$ 41.7	$ 364.6
Def. purchases	14.3	5.2	19.5	4.5	15.6	6.1	3.0	48.7
Defense %	85.1%	8.3%	24.6%	3.6%	43.9%	7.3%	7.2%	13.4%
1956 US total	$ 11.6	$ 78.7	$ 90.3	$135.1	$ 40.7	$101.6	$ 51.5	$ 419.2
Def. purchases	8.7	4.6	13.3	4.1	15.6	5.5	1.8	40.3
Defense %	75.0%	5.8%	14.7%	3.0%	38.3%	5.4%	3.5%	9.6%
1961 US total	$ 15.2	$ 81.3	$ 96.5	$165.8	$ 56.6	$142.9	$ 58.3	$ 520.1
Def. purchases	11.5	7.3	18.8	3.5	17.7	5.6	2.2	47.8
Defense %	75.7%	9.0%	19.5%	2.1%	31.3%	3.9%	3.8%	9.2%
1964 US total	$ 17.6	$109.4	$127.0	$192.4	$ 70.0	$174.2	$ 68.8	$ 632.4
Def. purchases	11.8	7.0	18.8	3.5	20.4	6.0	1.3	50.0
Defense %	67.0%	6.4%	14.8%	1.8%	29.1%	3.4%	1.9%	7.9%
1968 US total	$ 25.4	$149.1	$174.5	$255.0	$104.7	$241.9	$ 88.1	$ 864.2
Def. purchases	17.3	11.3	28.6	5.2	30.2	13.1	1.2	78.3
Defense %	68.1%	7.6%	16.4%	2.0%	28.8%	5.4%	1.4%	9.1%
1970 US total	$ 26.7	$153.5	$180.2	$288.1	$126.5	$283.8	$ 95.5	$ 974.1
Def. purchases	14.9	9.8	24.7	3.7	33.3	12.3	1.4	75.4
Defense %	55.8%	6.4%	13.7%	1.3%	26.3%	4.3%	1.5%	7.7%
1971 US total	$ 25.1	$168.6	$193.7	$300.5	$140.6	$303.1	$108.9	$1,046.8
Def. purchases	13.0	8.9	21.9	3.8	35.3	9.1	1.3	71.4
Defense %	51.8%	5.3%	11.3%	1.3%	25.1%	3.0%	1.2%	6.8%
1972 US total	$ 24.2	$195.3	$219.5	$317.2	$155.9	$325.1	$127.8	$1,145.5
Def. purchases	13.3	9.4	22.7	4.5	36.5	10.6	1.5	75.8
Defense %	55.0%	4.8%	10.3%	1.4%	23.4%	3.3%	1.2%	6.6%

While the 1972 defense shares shown above are the smallest since 1950, it is important to note that defense has not for many years had the dominant role that the military fundamentalists would ascribe to it. Here are the portions of the GNP allocated to defense for selected years:

NIA defense purchases as percent of:

Calendar years	Total GNP	Private sector output	Private sector output, less aircraft and ordnance
1953[a]	13.4%	10.1%	6.0%
1956	9.6%	6.5%	4.4%
1961	9.2%	6.5%	4.1%
1964	7.9%	5.3%	3.3%
1968	9.1%	6.3%	4.2%
1970	7.7%	5.0%	3.3%
1971	6.8%	4.0%	2.6%
1972	6.6%	4.0%	2.7%

a Note that these figures are for calendar year 1953. The figures for calendar year 1952, or for fiscal year 1953 (ending June 30, 1953) would show considerably higher percentages, since Korean War spending dropped sharply during calendar 1953. The FY 1953 or CY 1952 figures are not available on a comparable basis.

For reference, the 1972 figures just presented can be compared with the preceding text table. Table 7-5 presents data on these matters for selected years since 1953.

Setting aside aircraft and ordnance, then, defense purchases took about 4% of the private sector output through the post-Korea 1950's and 1960's, and are now taking less than 3%. It is a little hard to see how the defense 3% or 4% could have so thoroughly corrupted the other 96% or 97%.

Aircraft and ordnance. The aircraft and ordnance industries were mentioned earlier as areas where defense purchases clearly play a major role. As indicated in table 7-5, the defense share of the business in these industries has been in the 52-55% range since 1970, compared to 67-68% in the 1960's and 75-85% in the 1950's. While the defense share is dropping, it is still very large and has been large for a long time. Missiles and other military ordnance do not move in commercial markets, but aircraft do.

Recall the criticism that bad habits picked up through decades of dependence upon defense work had made American industry incompetent to compete in international markets, so that we find ourselves flooded with German and Japanese goods. The aircraft industry is surely one where it is possible to prove this point. It is heavily dependent upon defense work—some 20 times more so, on a relative basis, than American industry as a whole.

How does the American aircraft industry stack up? Have its products been pushed off the world markets? Are American airlines using German and Japanese aircraft? Not noticeably. As a matter of fact, Japan Air Lines is completely equipped with American planes. JAL had 64 air-craft in 1970—17 Boeing 727's, three 747's, 4 Convair 880's, and 40 DC-8's. As to the Germans, Lufthansa had 75 aircraft, of which 68 were American: a DC-4, 3 Boeing 747's, (20) 707's, (20) 727's, (24) 737's, and 7 Viscounts.[18] According to the Federal Aviation Administra-tion, there are no large German aircraft in use in this country and the only Japanese aircraft used is a small transport, the Nihon YS-11, of which there are 21 in the United States.

Moreover, the US aircraft industry has the largest favorable trade balance of any sector of American industry, including agriculture. In CY 1971, the US had an unfavorable trade balance (the first since 1888) of $2.9 billion. This was the net of a favorable balance of $3.0 billion for the aircraft industry, $1.4 billion for agriculture, and a net unfavorable balance of $7.3 billion for the remainder of American industry.

Thus this criticism fares very badly in an industry where defense has accounted for well over half of the business. Whatever is causing the other industries to have export problems, it clearly isn't defense. Per-haps the other 97.3% of the customers are creating the difficulty.

Electronics and shipbuilding are two other industries mentioned by critics for which we would like to have presented data. Unfortunately, the data available in the Departments of Commerce and Labor upon which the earlier GNP-related breakouts are based did not extend to shipbuild-ing on a comparable basis.

As to electronics, defense procurement accounts for about 19% of the total business—significant but not dominant.

Shipbuilding is mentioned as an industry that has been corrupted by defense work during recent decades. This is a particularly ill-founded charge. The fact is that the American shipbuilding industry has been in deep trouble, except in wartime, for almost a century. Following World War I, Alderfer and Michl note, "between 1922 and 1928, not a single transoceanic boat was launched in the United States."[19] Things

---

[18] *World Air Transport Statistics*, no. 15 (Geneva: International Air Transport Association, 1970), pp. 34 and 37.
[19] E. B. Alderfer and H. E. Michl, *Economics of American Industry* (New York: McGraw-Hill, 1942), pp. 133-134.

obviously didn't get much better in the 1930's, and the pattern was repeated after World War II. Max F. Millikan observed in 1950:[20]

> Compared to coal, steel, and agriculture, the ocean shipping industry represents but an insignificant sector of the American industrial framework. Here is an industry which, given the unfettered operation of the automatic market mechanism, would—except for the stimulus of periodic wars—have died three quarters of a century ago . . . Without artificial stimulation, the industry would have died simply because it has suffered from a comparative disadvantage in the international market, both in the construction and operation of ships.
>
> Ocean shipping is one of the things we Americans are not at the moment especially good at.

To point out that the shipbuilding industry is in trouble, then, is not exactly breaking new ground. To attribute these problems to defense procurement practices is simply inaccurate.

While the competitive problems of the American shipbuilding industry are a century old, it should be noted that the work performed for the US Navy is of outstanding quality. In the opinion of shipbuilding experts, the 688 class of nuclear submarines are probably the most splendid ships ever built. These submarines are understandably expensive because they required enormous capabilities and were built to rigorous standards of quality control. While costs may be high, there should be no implication that the US shipbuilding industry is incompetent to perform work of high quality.

On the commercial side, the US shipbuilding industry has recently begun to reverse the downward trends of the past several years. Since the President's shipbuilding program was enacted into law in 1970, over $1.1 billion in shipbuilding contracts have been awarded. Of this total, the Federal Government will pay about $479 million under the declining construction subsidy levels embodied in the Act. Prior to 1970, the Federal Government was assuming 55% of the total shipbuilding cost under subsidy contracts in accordance with the Construction Differential Subsidy. In FY 1973, this percentage will drop to 41%, thus indicating a sharp improvement in the ability of the American shipbuilding industry to move towards a more competitive position in world markets. Included in new shipbuilding contracts just announced are the three largest tankers (265,000 deadweight tons) ever to be built in the US, and the three largest roll-on roll-off van ships ever to be constructed in this

---

[20] In Walter Adams, *The Structure of American Industry* (New York: Macmillan, 1950), pp. 422-423.

country. This program has led to the construction or conversion of innovative, highly competitive ships for use in international commerce.[21]

Trends are completely ignored by some observers. Table 7-6 shows defense purchases of durable goods related to the US total in current prices and in constant (CY 1958) prices for selected *fiscal* years.[22] *The* trends come into sharp focus if we break the 33-year span into three 11-year periods:

	Final sales of durable goods in billions of CY 1958 dollars		
	US total	Defense	All other
FY 1939	$ 26.8	$ .4	$ 26.4
Increase, FY 1939 to FY 1950	+35.6	+2.6	+33.0
FY 1950	62.4	3.0	59.4
Increase, FY 1950 to FY 1961	+32.1	+12.5	+19.6
FY 1961	94.5	15.5	79.0
Increase, FY1961 to FY 1972	+75.6	+2.2	+73.4
FY 1972	170.1	17.7	152.4

Durable goods production for the civilian market grew $33 billion in constant prices, more than doubling, from 1939 to 1950. This involved moving from the deep depression year of 1939 (unemployment was 17.2%) to relatively prosperous 1950, with the massive stimulus of World War II along the way—pent-up demand and huge accumulations of savings. There was no such stimulus in the last 11 years, yet civilian sales of durable goods grew by $73.4 billion, nearly doubling, a truly phenomenal development.

During that span, defense purchase of durables grew just $2.2 billion. It is difficult to see how one can conclude that defense is dominating the durable goods market, or is starving the civilian sector for these goods.

It will be noted that defense did play a relatively large role over the decade of the 1950's. The defense increase itself was relatively large from FY 1950 to FY 1961, and total production of durable goods rose very slowly—especially from FY 1956 to FY 1961, as table 7-6 shows. The relatively small increase in production of durable goods for civilian markets over this period was largely a function of sluggish economic performance.

---

[21] President Nixon's Statement on *Maritime Affairs*, announced July 1 ,1972.
[22] We regret the need to shift from a calendar-year basis in Table 7-5 to a fiscal-year basis in Table 7-6. Key data used in Table 7-5 are available only on a calendar-year basis. The data used in Table 7-6 are available on either basis, but require complicated adjustments if a calendar-year basis is used, especially for 1950.

TABLE 7-6

US Sales of Durable Goods
($ in billions)

Final sales of durable goods

| Fiscal years | Current prices | | | Constant (CY 58) prices | | | Defense % of total |
	Total	Defense	All Other	Total	Defense	All Other	
1939	$12.4	$ .2	$12.2	$26.8	$ .4	$26.4	1.6%
1950	50.7	2.4	48.3	62.4	3.0	59.4	4.8
1953	76.0	29.6	46.4	86.2	33.5	52.7	38.9
1956	85.6	10.3	75.3	94.3	11.3	83.0	12.0
1961	95.8	15.7	80.1	94.5	15.5	79.0	16.4
1964	118.8	20.1	98.7	116.8	19.7	97.1	16.9
1968	162.0	28.5	133.5	151.2	26.6	124.6	17.6
1971	184.5	21.7	162.8	156.8	18.5	138.3	11.8
1972 Est.	203.2	21.2	182.0	170.1	17.7	152.4	10.4

High-technology industry. It is worthwhile to recall the trend in high-technology defense industry. Key data are as follows:

Department of Defense Prime Contract Awards in billions of CY 1958 dollars

(Fiscal year averages)

	FY 1958 −1961	FY 1962 −1965	FY 1967 −1968	FY 1971 −1972
Aircraft	$ 5.9	$ 5.4	$ 8.6	$ 5.5
Missile and space systems	4.4	5.6	4.1	3.6
Electronics and communications equipment	2.6	2.9	3.5	2.5
Educational and nonprofit institutions	.4	.6	.7	.6
Total, high technology	13.3	14.6	16.8	12.2
Other hard goods (including munitions)	3.0	4.4	9.4	5.2
Construction	1.3	1.2	1.0	.8
Soft goods and services	6.8	7.6	12.2	8.8
Total contract awards	24.4	27.8	39.4	27.0

Defense contracting in the high-technology area drops from an average of $13.3 billion per year in the 1958-61 period to $12.2 billion today. During this period, as we have seen, US technological capacity has grown immensely, as has US production of durable goods.

Soviet Political Warfare Techniques, Espionage and Propaganda in the 1970s by Lyman B. Kirkpatrick, Jr., and Howland H. Sargeant, January 1972

The Soviet Presence in the Eastern Mediterranean by Lawrence L. Whitten, September 1971

The Military Un*balance*
Is the U.S. Becoming a Second-Class Power? June 1971

The Future of South Vietnam by Brigadier F. P. Serong, February 1971 (Out of print)

Strategy and National Interests: Reflections for the Future by Bernard Brodie, January 1971

The Mekong River: A Challenge in Peaceful Development for Southeast Asia by Eugene R. Black, December 1970

Problems of Strategy in the Pacific and Indian Oceans by George G. Thomson, October 1970

Soviet Penetration into the Middle East by Wynfred Joshua, July 1970. Revised edition, October 1971

Australian Security Policies and Problems by Justus M. van der Kroef, May 1970

Detente: Dilemma or Disaster? by Gerald L. Steibel, July 1969

The Prudent Case for Safeguard by William R. Kintner, June 1969

Forthcoming

The Horn of Africa by J. Bowyer Bell, Jr.

The Soviet Presence in Latin America by James D. Theberge

The Development of Strategic Weapons by Norman Polmar

Contemporary Soviet Defense Policy by Benjamin S. Lambeth